The Resilience of a Gently Grown Man

Based on a true story

Sam Toller

Flowers of Purgatory—Conway, Arkansas
ISBN: 979-8-9902538-0-3
Library of Congress Control Number: 2024906588
Title: *The Resilience of a Gently Grown Man*
Author: Sam Toller
Digital distribution | 2024
Paperback | 2024

This is a work of fiction based on a true story. The characters, names, incidents, places, and dialogue are products of the author's imagination, and are not to be construed as real.

Dedication

I dedicate this book to my beautiful wife, Naomi. You have struggled through some of the most atrocious traumas a child could possibly face, and persevered into the wonderful mother and wife you are today. You are an inspiration to people everywhere who have high ACE scores, that coming through to the other side, is possible.

Part 1

Chapter 1
Tanna

I started this life in a world of incredible circumstances. My name is Tanna Lacey Parmstring, not the most common of names, though it isn't what I was given at birth. You see, I'm adopted— I was born and named Havana Lacey Rankle. I would start at the time I got adopted, but the story began far before then, it began around the first of the year, on the year that I was born. My biological parents are a greasy sort, both disgustingly sweet towards each other, but unwittingly dangerous towards their children. I was the first born of my parents, and they conceived me during the height of their drug induced romance. My bio-mother and bio-father did not know that I was rapidly developing and guiding the cells of my body into the shape that would become the infant born thirty-six weeks later. Even after finding out that my diminutive life as their little girl was rapidly approaching, my birth-mom did not stop the usage of her ever present, and favorite drug of choice, methamphetamine. You see, they were a chef of sorts, just not the culinary kind. Scientists of ill-repute, if you will. After I was born, I was given a drug test, not that I knew—I gained much of this information from my grandmother and aunts, but I failed that test. The doctors seemed to leap at the opportunity to get child protective services (CPS) involved, unfortunately for my biological parents, when CPS came into the room—they were literally putting flame to glass. Grandma was at the vending machine grabbing a snack and left me alone with my parents, she knew the kind of people they were. My parents knew that the nurse came in and checked on my mom and me once every hour to make sure we were doing good. It was all the opportunity they needed. Needless to say, CPS called the authorities, my father tried to run—and ultimately, my mom and dad were arrested.

I was put in my grandmother's care, but she was old, so it was a struggle for her, but she managed for a couple of years. My parents were released from jail after nine months and were in and out of my life. I didn't even know I had a little brother on the way, until CPS called my grandmother and informed her that my parents were sent to prison for manufacturing and disturbing narcotics, and my mom was 9 months pregnant. They asked if she would be able to care for a newborn baby, and of course she said yes, it was family. These first years flew by, and as I said, all the information I got came from the small snippets of gossip that was spewing from the narcissistic mouths of my aunts and grandmother.

After I was four years old, my grandmother became ill, not deathly ill, just too ill to care for a four-year-old and a two-year-old. She decided that I had learned enough from her and tried to place me into the adoption system. In order to prevent me from being put into the system, my aunt Selma took me in. She had a few other children, so one more wasn't a big deal.

A huge turning point for my, relatively normal life,

albeit rather sad, but normal for a child born in the streets of a drug legalized state, was my aunt Selma's boyfriend—Greg. You see, Greg had a thing for little girls, and it was insatiable. He often took my cousin Selena and me out to the woods and he would make us undress. Sometimes he would have us do things to each other while he fondled himself, and other times he wanted us both just for himself. I was six when the state took me away from them, six years old when I was put into the foster care system that fails so many children every year.

The funny thing is, I remember the foster homes more than I remember either of my grandmothers, or my aunts' home. I remember the abuse, and the anger those people had towards me, like I was a six-year-old inconvenience to them, sent to them to make their lives miserable. The first foster home, I felt, was just a forced labor camp. It was on a small rural farm, and I had to wake up super early, and do the most god-awful things. I'm sure some people think that it's a normal thing to be on a farm, and have to wake up and do things, but this was all day, and I was six, and I was a girl. I had to use a huge fat flat shovel to scrape chicken shit off the floor of a small wooden shack filled with little boxes. At the time, I had no idea they were roost nests for the hens to lay their eggs. I never got to gather the eggs, that was Sydney's job, she was the foster home's biological daughter, she got everything she wanted. I had to do the dishes at the house every single day, three times a day. Mrs. K would not make a meal in a dirty kitchen, no ma'am. I was there for two entire months before the foster system swooped in to transport me into another home, that appeared perfect

4

on the surface.

Foster home number two, only lasted two days. Mr. Frank put me into the hospital because I didn't bring him his coffee fast enough. I was hit so hard in the head with a rolled-up magazine, I was given a concussion and eight stitches where I smashed my face into the table. Last I heard, the state was going to take care of him, whatever that means.

Foster home number three was relatively calm. It was an elderly couple, whose kids were grown, and was just doing their civil duty to their country, by taking in the children of ill reputable pasts. They took decent care of me, and sometimes I wonder how those sweet old folks were doing, but I'm certain they have probably passed, as they were indeed incredibly old.

Chapter 2
Adopted

I was adopted a short time after I turned seven years old. I never quite understood why anyone would want to adopt me. Even at seven years old, I didn't think that I was "worthy" of being adopted, I was damaged goods, from a damaged background, and used up by an over-weight bald man in the backwoods of Washington state. Why would these seemingly nice and wealthy people want a little girl, who had nothing to offer them?

The incredibly nice and wealthy family that adopted me wanted another child around the house after their older children grew up and became thriving contributing members to society. Franny and Gus seemed like very sweet people, although the way they started our relationship was by telling me I would no longer be Haven Lacey, that my new name would be Tanna Lacey Parmstring. I didn't want that; I liked my name. It irked me to my soul that I didn't even have a say in what I would be called. I didn't much care for the name Tanna, but it became a foundation of who I am today. Franny and Gus, or should I say, "mom and dad," were successful business owners, and they worked very hard for the things they got. They owned a few businesses in a small town in Arkansas where I moved to. As it was that they had indeed adopted me, this home would be my forever home.

I was given practically anything I wanted, I was just expected to clean up around the house while mom and dad were at work. I also had to watch the dogs, I had a small poodle of my own, and mom and dad had one each of their own too. We lived in a beautiful home on top of a hill that overlooked the small city, that I would one day roam, seeking to fill a void that could never be filled.

Everything started out fairly well. I had doctor appointments to make sure I was healthy, and thriving, I had appointments set up with therapists, so they could check and make sure my mind was good… I didn't much care for them, they always tried to make me seem like I was broken. I wasn't broken, everyone else was. My mom and dad liked to take me on little trips around the United States and sometimes Mexico. I was given the very best of everything, and taught appropriate manners, and how to get my way.

By the time I was ten, I was all joy, just wobbling about and being silly. My dad very quickly became my favorite. Gus had a big soft spot for me in his heart, I could get away with murder. People always say that a father's little girl held his entire world in her precious little hands. This statement was absolutely true for my father, as it was for so many other girls around the world. We went to church twice a week, and most of the family friends were God-fearing individuals who had money. We didn't associate much with those of the lesser class, though I never heard my parents speak ill of them, they were decent people after all.

I met my first boyfriend at church, he was a sweet kid, and he gave me so many compliments. He really liked how I looked, being just shy of eleven years old, I had begun to show my womanly body, and he just couldn't get enough of it. He was fourteen. We would sneak behind the bushes and shrubbery that surrounded the trees and experiment with each other, it wasn't love, who even knew what love was or how it felt at that age? All I know is it felt really good when he called me beautiful, and I wanted to hear him say that all the time.

One Wednesday night at Church, Sebastian didn't show up, he was sick. I knew his friend liked to tease me and eyeballed his best friend enviously, so I invited him to the bushes. It only made sense to me, we were young, I didn't have to be tied down to anyone, even if he told me he loved me all the time. I knew how to get what I wanted, and what I wanted was to be told I was pretty. Jefferson wasn't the most all-together boy, he was a little delayed, but I didn't mind, this made it easier for me to get him to do what I wanted. My mom caught us tonight, only because Jefferson's little sister Abigale saw us going into the bushes and spied on us. She ran to the adults screaming: "Tanna and Jefferson are kissing in the bushes!" I probably would have heard her if Jefferson wasn't such a fat lousy mouth-breather, breathing super scruffily in my ears while he pawed and scratched at my legs. I didn't though, and my mom showed up and whisked me away, asking me what the heck I was doing.

That was the last night I went to that church. That was the last night I thought about Sebastian or Jefferson for a very long time. They didn't matter anyway, just a couple of boys. I went to see my therapist the next day. I told her that it felt good that these boys liked how I looked and gave me compliments. I didn't see a problem with it, every girl should be told they were beautiful and pretty. I even asked my therapist if anyone had told her she was pretty lately, because it would be a shame if they hadn't. She wasn't pretty of course, but once again, I knew how to get what I wanted. My mom wasn't so easy to manipulate or get what I wanted from her. She would yell at me and tell me I was being bad. When I told the Therapist that my mom was yelling at me all the time for no reason at all, she brought mom in, and we discussed it. Needless to say, dear old Franny started looking for another therapist the next day.

A couple more years went by, and things started to go downhill rapidly with my parents. I would really hash it out with my mom, and my dad started to drink heavily. He would have six whole beers every day. Then he would sit there and brood until bedtime, listening to my mom and I shouting at each other. I had finally gotten a cell phone and my mom was mad at me for talking all night to one of my friends. This time, I told her I was sorry, and it wouldn't happen again. Fortunately, it placated her for a little while, which was good because we had a trip to Virginia coming up, just us girls.

On our plane ride, we joked and giggled, and enjoyed our snacks up in first class. It was really fun. When we got to Virginia, the first night we walked around and explored the different historical monuments and various art displays that the universities put out. The second night was the night that the entire world really changed for me.

This wonderful night I experienced the power, and

taste of a man. My mom decided she wanted to go to the casino and bar and get her a couple of drinks, so she left me in the room, alone. I hopped onto social media and started searching the local areas for people wanting to meet up. I found a man and invited him over to my hotel room. He was thirty years old; I was fourteen.

This was the first time I actually experienced a man with my full unadulterated consent. A lot of people think that I can't give consent because I'm just a "child," but I knew how to get what I want, and this was what I wanted right then. Thinking back, I think I know better. I know that a kid cannot 'really' give consent, I know that kids are sporadic and full of inhibition. I just don't really care, I go after what I want, and I will always get it.

As kids do, and I wasn't quite as proficient in being sneaky as I am today, I lost track of time. My mom came into the room and found me there, without clothes and with condom trash lying about on the floor. I wasn't stupid, I made sure a condom was used, I knew I wasn't on birth control at the time. Fortunately, the man had left a little bit before, or it could have gone much, much worse. She still went absolutely ballistic. I mean, what did she expect, leaving a girl alone for several hours. If anything, it was her fault for what happened, not mine.

My mom became exceptionally controlling after the Virginia incident. She had my cell phone completely locked down… and I mean completely. She had all the parental controls in place, I couldn't add a friend to my contact list without her permission. I couldn't download a game application without her giving me

10

the side eye, when I asked her to put her password in, to grant me permission. We went to church a couple times a week still, and she increased the number of times I went to the therapist. I wasn't allowed to go anywhere or do anything.

Chapter 3
Sixteen

It was fall when I turned 16 years old. My mom was taking me to my seventh different therapist. Most of the therapists I just made feel super uncomfortable and then they referred us to another one. It's a bit unusual, considering that's literally their job, dealing with unfortunate minds. This therapist was my latest, and greatest ally. She would side with me, when I would tell her about the things my mom would keep me from, and why she kept them from me. I didn't tell the truth about a lot of it, but why should I? I know how to get what I want. The therapist even had to call the "child protective service hotline" number a couple of times, because of how my mom was controlling everything I did. Nothing ever came of it, but why would it? I was a Mexican girl who was adopted by an incredibly wealthy, white family.

My mom recorded a video of me following her around the house, screaming and cussing her out. I was incredibly offended; she didn't portray anything about "WHY" I was cussing her out. I do say, I looked incredible on camera though. I never would have had to yell at her, if she didn't take my phone away because I snuck off to see my boyfriend instead of going to work. I liked to swap days with my coworkers, so I could go to "work," and then go see my man. He loved to tell me how beautiful I was, and my mom had me on birth control since the Virginia incident, so everything should have been perfectly fine. His parents caught us, sneaking about, and told my mom and dad about it. We went to church together, his family was wealthy, and white. What more could they have wanted for me? So what if I was skipping out on work and school to do what I wanted, I didn't need anyone or anything telling me what to do, I knew how to get everything I wanted.

My boyfriend broke up with me, because his parents said that he wasn't allowed to date or even be in any relationship. That's okay, because Kyle went to church with us, and my mom and dad liked him. They even let him be in my phone contact list, because he was "of a good sort" as my dad liked to say. He had plans to go into the military this summer, he had big plans to be able to provide for mine and his futures. He thought I was cute too. My ex-boyfriend had no idea that I was already talking to Kyle, and have been since the day my mom let him be in my phone. I don't talk with him on the traditional messenger or texting apps because my mom watched those closely. I got him set up in another app that kids and adults used to talk to each other about gaming.

My mom and dad let me become Kyle's girlfriend a couple weeks later. It was nice, he would come over and hang out with my dad and me, and I would be allowed to go on some 'supervised' dates with him, like to the movies. It was still under a lot of control and oppression, but that was okay, I knew it was just a matter of time before I could push and get what I wanted.

The night came in late May. My mom and I got into

a particularly big fight. I wanted to hit my mom so bad. My parents told me to stand out on the porch and cool down, so I went and stood outside fuming. I managed to grab my phone, which was nice. After twenty minutes, I tried to go back inside, to find the door locked. I pounded, and pounded, screaming that I was going to burn the house down if they didn't let me back inside. It was all to no avail. I smiled when I thought of a plan, so I called my friend Felicia to come get me, so I could stay at her house. When I got there, I texted Kyle and told him to come get me. You see, I never intended on staying at Felicia's house, but instead with Kyle. I knew my mother was tracking my phone, so I had to go to Felicia's house to drop my phone off, and then have Kyle come get me. I was going to get exactly what I wanted.

After a few days, Kyle told me I had to leave, that his parents weren't ok with me staying there. So, I went back to Felicia's house, and called my mom. I told her I was sorry; I wasn't. She let me come home, under the stipulation that I had an extra session with my therapist, which was fine with me. I didn't tell my therapist everything, because she would begin to side with my mom if I did, but I paid close enough attention to what I did tell her, so she wasn't able to catch me in a lie. Every now and then, she would eye me suspiciously, but I was unyielding, and didn't cave.

Kyle went off to basic training, he still had his senior year in high school to finish, and I was utterly devastated. I wrote letters every single day. My mom and dad made sure to provide me with lots and lots of stamps so I could send him all the letters I could possibly have wanted. He made me feel so lonely, being gone for that long, I could barely hold myself together. I felt myself crying all the time, which was nice, because my mom and dad would baby me when I cried. I knew deep down that this was another weapon I could utilize, to get everything I wanted.

When Kyle returned from basic training, he came over to my house and hugged me and told me he loved me. I looked stunning in his big, fit, muscular arms. I was a perfect complement to his military toned body. I don't know what hurt me the most when he left, the fact that I had spent so much time planning our future together, or the fact that he left me because he was getting attention from girls, that he found prettier. I knew that for a dumb guy, he had a great body, and was tall. He would get all sorts of attention from different girls, or boys, I cared not for what he desired. Tomorrow was homecoming, he broke up with me yesterday, but I wasn't going to let him put me down, I knew how to get what I wanted.

Part 2
The Gently Grown Man

Chapter 4
Homecoming

'*U*h, the best livin' or dead hands down, huh less talk, more head right now, huh*' by Kanye West* was thumping in the background, while I danced and gyrated on the bodies of my friends who were around me. The lights were flashing, and the crowd of young adults were whooping and hollering in glee and joy as the homecoming dance pressed on. I looked around for someone I knew could fill the void I had, no matter how I flirted or rubbed against my friends, I was unable to get the compliments and affirmations I wanted, so I had to settle for finding someone who would give me those things. I noticed a boy sitting by himself, in blue-jeans and a relatively nice shirt, near the snack bar. He was just quietly munching and bobbing along with the music, being quiet and completely satisfied with being alone. From my past experiences, I knew that he was the kind of boy I could get to do anything I wanted.

"He's sooooooo cute!" I whisper-yelled into the ear of Kaylee one of my best friends.

"Who!?" she yelled back.

"Him!" I practically screamed, as I pointed out the boy sitting at the snack bar.

"Ooooooh, he IS really cute! I'm going to go talk to him!" Kaylee giggled and started to head towards the boy.

"I think NOT!" I snatched her arm, almost too roughly, and jerked her back towards me. "I saw him first, I'm going to go talk to him!"

"Fine! Ugh, I call the next one though."

I made my way over to the boy, just looking at him at first. Studying him, while he sat there and picked at the chips and occasionally sipped on a red plastic cup. He was REALLY cute, with dark brown hair, freshly cut. A strong jawline, and a perfectly proportional face. I couldn't tell the color of his eyes, in the dark, but I imagined them as a bright blue, or a dark green. He was thin, in shape but not overly muscular. I could tell he was tall, taller than Kyle. He would be perfect to make Kyle jealous. This was the guy that held the keys to everything I wanted, and I was going to take them from him.

"Eh hem, Hi, I'm Tanna, can I sit next to you?" I asked nervously, putting on a little more nervous quiver than was necessarily required. I would have to do better.

"Oh, hi, uh, yeah, sure," he said, obviously nervous. I couldn't tell if he had ever spoken to a girl before or not, and it got me even more excited. He stood up, and I noticed immediately he was much taller than I had anticipated, probably over six feet tall. He gestured softly towards a chair next to the one he was standing in front of.

"Please, after you, can I go grab you a drink?" His baritone voice was gentle, and strong. His kindness surprised me, and the manners! I nodded, and sat down, when he walked over to the drink table and grabbed me a drink in a red plastic cup. He also grabbed a small shiny plastic plate and added a little bit of the cookies and chips that were on the table. Sitting down next to me, he placed the plate and drink on the table in between the two of us. He gazed at me, and when the lights swept over us, I caught a glimpse of his eyes, they were a deep green. He smelled like a freshly mown lawn in the soft breeze of a crisp fall day. I was mesmerized for a moment and almost lost my nerve right then but steadied myself with the resolve of a woman on a mission. I was going to get what I wanted, and nothing was going to stop me.

"What's your name?" I questioned.

"My name is Zebadiah Ethan Fowler, but people just call me Zeb, in fact—That's what I prefer."

"Well then, hi there Zeb, my name is Tanna Lacey Parmstring, but people just call me Tanna." I giggled and flirted sweetly with my eyes.

I leaned forward pushing my cleavage out a little, so it was very noticeable. I tried to draw attention to some of my easiest to use weapons, in a one-sided battle, but I could not get him to look down, at all. He kept his gaze on my face, never straying except to glance at the crowd from time to time to make sure no one was spinning or dancing too close. Almost like he was keeping vigil and standing firm in an unknown duty to guard and protect those weaker or smaller than him.

"You're as smooth as Tennessee Whiskey.... You're as sweet as Strawberry wine...." by Chris Stapleton played in the background as we continued our conversation.

"Tell me about yourself, what's your favorite color? How old are you? When is your birthday? What do you like to do? Where were you born? Do you like to watch movies?" I asked in a whirlwind of cliches.

'Don't seem to eager Tanna, just be yourself, you're perfect, he's going to like you no matter what,' I told myself, as I sat there trying to get this boy to show me a little bit of the normal hormone-fueled desires a teenage boy usually displays.

He chuckled and answered, "My favorite color is red, I turned 18 years old in September, I really love playing video games, I was born in Alaska, and of course I like movies, who doesn't?" After a breath, he asked quietly, "How about you?"

"Well, there isn't much to tell, except a lot." I laughed, hoping he would get my awkward joke. "I'm adopted, my parents rule my world with an iron fist, I'm lucky that I even got to go to this homecoming dance. I was adopted when I was seven years old, my favorite color is purple, I was born in Washington state. My favorite types of movies are horror films, because I like to snuggle up with someone while they hold me, as we both get scared.

"As I said though, my name is Tanna Lacey, though I was born as Havana, my parents changed my name when I got adopted. You were born in Alaska!? That's incredible, I've always wanted to go to Alaska, I hear it's super beautiful. Do you remember much of it?" I was starting to get a little nervous jabber-tongue going on, so I bit down on my tongue to stop it.

"I don't remember a whole lot of it, I left there when I was four. I do remember it being really cold outside," he answered then took a long drink of punch from his cup.

We went into a small awkward silence for a little while, neither of us knowing exactly what to say to each other, but simply enjoying each other's company. I've never faced someone who completely ignored my physical assets and just looked at me. It was a little scary, almost like he was looking directly into my soul.

After about five minutes of us enjoying the music and drinking our punch, I asked him, "So, do you have a girlfriend?"

He shook his head. "Nope, I don't care much about being in relationships, and I'm not big on the touchy-feely stuff. So, I just avoid the relationship stuff because I feel like I would not have a lot to offer someone."

"I'm sure you have a lot to offer, for instance, you're tall, handsome, do you work? Do you have a car? What grade are you in? I've seen you around the school, but there's a lot of kids that go here, so I don't remember exactly where I've seen you," I questioned.

"I don't know," he said with a small smile. "I do work, it's my favorite thing to do. I work for the human development center, in the maintenance department. I don't make a lot of money, but I make enough, considering I still live at home with my parents, and I ride a motorcycle."

He gestured towards a leather jacket I hadn't noticed, hanging behind his chair. "Though my parents did tell me I was going to get a vehicle for graduation. I'm a senior…if you hadn't gathered that bit from all that."

My eyes widened a bit when I realized that he wasn't kidding, he worked, he was older, he had a motorcycle, and he was about to graduate? '*My goodness, I would get all sorts of attention by dating him. I've got to figure out how to do that,*' I thought to myself.

"What do you like to do for fun? I like to play volleyball and sing, I've been in choir since I was like three years old, so I'd say I'm a pretty good singer. Also, I just really love volleyball." I glanced around and realized the noise was really loud in the building. "Do you want to move our conversation outside to sit on the bench walls by the pathways?"

"Uhh Sure." He stood up, and grabbed his jacket, and immediately headed towards the doors, leaving me still sitting there. He turned and looked back at me, with a small, crooked smile on his face, almost beckoning me onwards with his gaze. As he got to the door, he held it for me, even though I was a short way behind him. I thought it was oddly gentlemanly of him to hold the door for me, knowing I was coming. I put a little pep in my step to catch up to him. I felt somewhat in shock at the treatment he was giving me, I felt like he only had eyes for me—like his entire mission in life was to please me. I lived for this feeling.

When we got outside into the courtyard, he led us towards a short two-foot wall that surrounded the area, and guided students along the pathways. The grass was still green but was starting to fade to that yellowish brown that signified fall was surely at our doorstep. The air was cool, but not terribly cold, in Arkansas it doesn't get too cold until around Christmas or after the new year. The moon was full and only the brightest stars could be seen, because of how much light pollution was present in that small school courtyard.

"What time do you have to be home? My parents make me be home by ten, and they literally control everything about my life. I'm not allowed to put anyone in my phone or download any app I want. Everything is under tight supervision and controlled by my mother?" I asked with a complaining tone.

"My parents don't give me a curfew, they trust me. They know I'm not going to go out and do stupid things. I haven't ever given them a reason not to trust me, so it works out well," he said as a matter of fact.

I didn't get the impression he was mocking me or pointing out that I had indeed given my parents reason not to trust me. I felt more like he was making it a statement of fact, because that's exactly what it was. I wondered briefly how that must feel, having all the freedom in the world with no one second guessing my decisions. It must be amazing.

"Really?! That must be nice, I think I've been under lock and key and stuck in a tower since I was seven years old. You see, my parents own a few businesses here, so it's not outside of their means to buy everything in the world that could allow them to keep track of exactly where I'm at and what I'm doing at all times." I considered him for a moment as he stared up at the moon. "Hey Zeb, you said you didn't have a girlfriend... would you consider letting me be your girlfriend?"

There was a few moments of quiet silence, not uncomfortable, just like that hushed sound before the curtains fell after a play had ended. I was nervous, because for the first time in my life, I wasn't sure if the boy I was speaking to would give me the answer I was seeking. It irked me to no end, that I may have come up against someone, who actually wanted more than what I had to offer.

"Yeah, sure." His eyes looked nervously at the

ground, almost embarrassed. "I'd really like that, I do want to let you know though, I don't do touching. I just can't stand someone's skin touching my own, it's like fingernails going down a chalkboard. It's like chewing on a cotton ball. It's like the feeling of having aluminum scrape between your teeth or having dust on your fingertips and then rubbing your fingertips together. It sends gooseflesh up and down my spine, and makes me quiver with… with… I don't even know what it's called. Do you think that will be an issue?"

"Zeb! Of course, that won't be an issue. Touching other people is gross! That's not my cup of tea at all. I tell you what I'll do, I'll ask your permission before I even give you a hug, is that okay?"

"I'd like that a lot, thank you for respecting my space," he said sweetly.

The time was quickly approaching nine-thirty, and I knew I would have to be leaving soon, so we started walking the short walk to where I'd parked my car.

"Can I give you a hug Zeb?"

Instead of answering with an affirmative, he wrapped his long arms around my small body, and pulled me into an embrace. It was sweet, and for a moment, I thought we were going to kiss. After what felt like mere seconds, he released me.

"Be careful on your way home Tanna," he said quietly. "I'll see you at school on Monday."

"You be careful too Zeb. That bike is crazy unsafe at night." I climbed into my car and started it. "I'll see you at school," I said out the window, as I creeped away in my small compact car. A smile was on my face because I knew without a shadow of a doubt that I had no reason to question my capabilities earlier. I got

24

exactly what I wanted because all the boys were the same. I'm going to break this one, his perfect world, the perfect trust his parents give him. I'm going to make Kyle jealous and reject him. It was just a matter of time, but I knew how to get what I wanted.

Chapter 5
Birthday Party

"He's been super sweet, but I don't get to see him often, he doesn't get to school until after 8 am and he leaves before lunch, to go to work." I was telling one of my best friends Sadie on the phone a couple days later.

"Gurrrrl, he is sooo cute! There's no telling how you ever managed to pull a guy like that, with you out here looking like an Oompa Loompa, I wonder if he wants a real woman instead," Sadie teased.

"You wish! My mom is trying to make me not look like an Oompa Loompa, she controls everything I eat, that's why I keep getting Kyle and JP to buy me food every day. Girl JP is so hot; I've always had a crush on him," I said wistfully, staring off into outer space.

"You better stop! You got a mans! I mean if you don't want him, I'll take him off your hands…"

"Hmph! You couldn't take him from me if you tried, but you won't because you love me."

Sadie looked at me and offered some advice, "Yeah, I do, seriously though, you should treat him good, he seems like a really good one."

I rolled my eyes and made some excuses to get off the phone. "Alright, I'm going to hop off the phone, I've got to take my dog for a walk, let him shit all over the yard. Bye Sadie! I love you babe!"

"Love you too Tanna! See you at school tomorrow!"

After we got off the phone, I looked at my little brown toy goldendoodle, and rolled my eyes again. I figured that I would take him out in a bit and went to the mirror. It was a full-faced mirror, that allowed me to look at my entire body. I was short, five foot tall, with dark brown hair, and burnt coffee-colored eyes. I had a mole on my forehead that stood out, my mom and dad would not let me get it removed. I was light skinned for being a Latin American girl, with quite a bit of extra weight around my midriff. My mom and dad didn't know that I liked to sneak a lot of snacks at night, not to mention what I got the boys to buy me at school. My teeth were very straight, as the result of thousands of dollars that my parents put into my dental work, but they couldn't pay enough to make me take care of them. They were yellowing more and more every day, probably the result of smoking on a vape, drinking large quantities of coffee and soda, and not brushing my teeth but once or twice a week. I knew better, I just didn't care. I may have been a petit plus size girl, but I knew how to carry myself, and I knew how to make every guy want me.

My dog made a small whimpering sound, while standing by the door. I knew he wanted to go out, he probably really needed to go out bad. I stared at him for a few more moments, thinking about just how needy he was being. I mean sheesh, I gave him everything, his home, his bed, his little clothes, and his food. Well, my parents paid for all of it, but that's just the same as me giving it to him.

"Ugh! Fine I'll take you out, fuck you're needy." I grabbed one of my many hoodies that I've collected

27

over the years from all the different boys I've teased and threw it on. I snatched the dog's leash off of the hooks by the door and lashed it around the dog's neck roughly.

"Let's go Hanky-poo, let's go outside. You got to go potty?!" I "baby-talked" to my dog like he was my child. He bounced around and yipped softly, because of me giving him a little attention. Dogs were so thirsty for attention, always waiting and bouncing around when they got the smallest bit of attention. I glared at my dog in disgust but still spoke in the high-pitched voice of someone who is speaking like a baby to a dog, "Damn you're such a stupid dog, come on, let's go outside you stupid dog."

I took my dog out the front door and walked towards the grass, across our very long and sloped driveway. We lived at the top of a big hill that overlooked the city, in a very large home. It was way more than what we needed, but my parents liked to splurge and show off how much they had, so I went with it. I was supposed to carry a plastic doggy-poo bag when I walked the dog, but I was not going to do that. I was not going to pick up poop, because that's just nasty.

After Hank did his deed, I took him back into the house and put him inside. My birthday was in a few days, so I figured I'd see if I could get people to come to my birthday party. There was a new entertainment facility across town, so I sat down in the rocking chair on the front porch, and started texting, getting RSVPs from several of my girlfriends. I wanted to see if Kyle still had feelings for me, so I figured I'd text him too.

-Me: Hey, what are you doing?

-Kyle: Nothing much, just chilling with my dad.

What about you?

-Me: Planning my birthday party, we are doing it at O'Shallys.

-Kyle: That's cool.

-Me: Yeah, I wanted to have it somewhere that was new and neat…

-Me: So….

-Me: Do you want to come?

-Me: I mean you don't have to, but it would be nice if you did.

-Me: For old times' sake.

-Me: Hello? You there?

-Kyle: Yeah, I'm here. Was just thinking… Don't you have a boyfriend?

-Me: Yeah but he doesn't have to know, he won't be there.

-Kyle: That's kind fucked up, but… I'm down for it.

-Me: Cool! It'll be at 5:30. I'll see you there.

I smiled satisfactorily. I knew he'd come. Why wouldn't he? I'm pretty amazing. It proves that he still wants me, he just wanted a little strange after getting out of basic training. That's totally understandable, I liked a little strange from time to time too, well all the time, but yeah.

During school the next day, I got an amazing surprise when I got off the bus. There was Zeb. He was standing there with his crooked smile, looking at me. I ran to him and hugged him. He awkwardly hugged me back.

"What are you doing here!?"

"I know I don't have to go to class until eight-thirty, but I wanted to see you, so I got up early and came to school at…" he glanced at his watch, "seven-fifteen."

"That is the sweetest thing! Wow you really are a great catch!"

He blushed and gave me a small smile. With the weather starting to turn, we headed towards the cafeteria to sit down for a little while. He held each door for me, which was nice. It always confused me how some people feel insulted when a man opens or holds a door for them, I feel like that's how it should be, after all, us women do rule the world. Men should serve us. It's nice that he is chivalrous and kind, it does makes me smile and feel good.

"So…my birthday is in a couple of days, my parents aren't going to let me spend it with anyone but a couple of girlfriends, they said I'm not allowed to date anyone either, so that's why I can't invite you over. I'm really sorry, my parents are such jerks," I lied easily.

With the sides of his lips slightly turned down, sadly, he said, "It's okay, what do you want to eat? I'll buy you lunch on your birthday; I'll just take off quickly and grab you something, then bring it back to you before going to work."

"Hmm… Let me think of something close, so you don't risk being late for work. I do like Juan Pepe's. Would that be okay?"

"Works for me, I like their burritos too."

A couple days later, my birthday was upon us. I went to school as normal, and Zeb was there. I hopped off the bus and bounced over to him, a big smile on my face. He had a huge smile on his face too, and when I asked him if I could hug him, he opened his arms and took me in. He was serious about his aversion to human contact, I don't know what happened to him growing up, that he couldn't stand the touch of another person, but I understood that sometimes, things that happened as a child, were better left buried deep.

At lunch, Zeb ran over to Juan Pepe's, and grabbed me a burrito. This place was sort of like a food court line, where you walk in front of a window where there were several people standing at a station. They asked what sort of beans you wanted on your burrito, what sort of meat, and cheese and vegetables. It was really good. After he returned and delivered me the burrito he purchased, and some bags of candy, that he knew were my favorite, he had to dart off to work. I smiled as I watched him rush off to his motorcycle.

"Tanna, you're going to destroy that boy," Sadie said softly, standing by my side. She knew how I handled the boys in my life, she knew that I liked things my way. "He doesn't deserve any of that... You may just be his very first girlfriend, with how sweet and kind he is."

"Pshh, I'm not going to destroy him, he won't ever find out about anything I do. Kyle is coming to my birthday party today. I may be able to get my parents to let him give me a ride." I smiled sweetly.

"Kyle has a girlfriend! Trish is your friend!" Sadie gasped.

"Trish WAS my friend, but she isn't anymore. She put out to Kyle the first day they got together. That's the only reason he left me for her."

"That's just gross."

"I know right."

That evening, I asked my parents if Kyle could pick me up and take me to get a slushy from the local ice cream store, before we met them at O'Smally's at 5:30.

"Yes, but we will not abide you being a second late," my mother warned, unspoken threats looming behind her words.

"I won't be, I promise."

-Me: Kyle, come get me now and take me to get a slushy. DTF.

-Kyle: Be there in five.

-Me: K.

Kyle picked me up and we drove down the hill towards the city. It wasn't quite dark yet, though the darkness was battling with the remaining vestiges of sunlight. We pulled through a quick slushy drive-through, and he pulled off the road into a quiet parking lot to talk.

"We have to make this quick, my parents will not 'abide me being one second late,'" I said sarcastically and rushed, stripping out of my clothes.

"I can do that." He chuckled, undoing his pants.

Exactly forty-five seconds later, I was grumpily pulling my clothes back on, he was sighing and breathing heavily. With a sour smile on my face, I told him, "Get your clothes back on, we've got to go."

"Of course, princess, we will be there in time, you know I still love you right? I just can't be with you right now; Trish is not as controlled by her parents as you are."

I grimaced, "I know you do, it's alright, we are both taken right now."

The party went off without a hitch. We made it on time, and played games and did a little bowling with my family and the girls. I found myself thinking about Zeb from time to time, wondering if he would have shown up, if I had invited him. I don't think my parents would have liked him to come, they still hoped I would end up with Kyle. Kyles' parents had money, and they were friends with my parents. It would really crinkle their craw if they knew that I would never end up with Kyle, I knew he still wanted me though, I just had to reject him, when the time was right. I knew how to get what I wanted, sometimes it just took a little time.

Chapter 6
Locked Out

The day after my birthday, I had school. Zeb met me as I got off the bus, so he could hang out with me for a little time before classes started. We started talking about our home life, and I complained about how controlling my parents were.

"I'm literally not allowed to do anything. My dad drinks all the time, like four or five beers a day, and he yells at me all the time. My mom follows me around the house complaining about the things I do, or what they say I don't do. It's really not fair," I whined the last little bit, with a little extra drag on the words really and fair.

He winced and empathized with what I was saying, "Dang Tann, that's the worst. I'm sorry you have to live that way. If there was something I could do, I'd totally do it. I mean my parents aren't controlling in the least, other than making me take the trash out, do the dishes occasionally, and change the litter boxes. We have three cats, so that's kind of a full-time job, but even then, they don't really yell at me if I forget, just remind me to get it done immediately, when I do."

He paused for a moment considering, thinking about some of the worst situations that I had to go through, but not knowing the absolute worst of the worst. I hadn't told him yet, I figured I would eventually, when

I wanted to get something for it. Everything had a price; I usually knew what to use as payment.

"Well, only a year left until you turn eighteen. If things go good for us, we can at least see that there's light at the end of the tunnel," he said with a small smile on his face.

"Yeah, at least there's that," I said quietly as he walked me to my first class. We walked in silence for a little while, and I considered how to get what I wanted. I wanted the freedom he had, the lack of control, the access to junk food and the space to do exactly what I wanted at all times. I just wasn't sure how to make that happen, what I was sure about was that I did not want to wait a year to get it.

That evening, I was lying on the couch, watching one of those hot guy reality tv shows on a beach somewhere. Everyone is banging everyone else, drinking, partying, and ultimately having a good time. I could easily imagine myself in one of those scenarios, where all the guys were vying for my attention, trying to get me to accept them. I'd play them all, it wouldn't even be that hard.

My little dog jumped up on the couch while I was mid-daydream and disturbed my thoughts. I glared at him, gave him a little kick to his ribs to get him off the couch, and yelled at him, "Dammit Hank! Why are you always... around!"

He whimpered at me, then cowed in place, and left a small puddle on the floor. I rolled my eyes and went back to watching the television. I knew I'd have to clean it up, but I'd do it when I got good and ready to do it. No sooner had I got that thought out of my mind than my mom and dad walked through the front door.

My mom took one look at me, sprawled out on the couch, watching 'smut,' with a plate sized wet spot on the hardwood floors right in front of the couch, and then started yelling at me.

"Are you seriously just going to lay there and not clean up after your dog? You're going to neglect your dog and not take him out when he needs to use the restroom? I guarantee you that he was whining so you could take him out, you probably just ignored him! Get off your butt and clean that up then take him outside!"

I rolled my eyes and took in a deep breath to start a hastily concocted lie, "He didn't whine at all, I had fallen asleep and just woke up when you guys walked into the house, I didn't know."

My mom looked at me with disbelieving eyes, I knew she knew I was lying, but she was calculating on whether it was worth it to fight with me tonight or not. "Just clean it up."

I figured, since she was in a giving mood and not wanting to fight with me today, I should capitalize on this and bring up Zeb to her. Step one of my plan was to get her to let me add his phone number into my phone. He gave me his number, I had it written down. I was told to use it if I ever needed to talk to him, he was available. He understood that I was not able to give him my number because Ursella would never allow it. I sometimes called my mom Ursella comparing her to the evil octopus on *The Little Mermaid*, it gave me a small chuckle every time I did.

"Hey mom, so… I got a boyfriend… his name is Zeb. He's super sweet and nice, I think you guys would really like him. Can I put his phone number in my phone and text him? Maybe he can come by sometime and you and dad can meet him?"

"Oh no, absolutely not. You and I both know that you'll just end up with Kyle again, running around and carrying on. There's no way I'm going to let you hurt another innocent boy!"

"I'm not going to end up with Kyle again, we didn't run around and carry on with anything. That's gross mom! I wouldn't do anything like that ever! I'm saving myself for marriage, just like you told me to," I lied smoothly.

"My answer is still no. I don't want to deal with this today. We will be having dinner shortly, so please go clean yourself up," she said as she continued to shuffle around the kitchen, making dinner.

I stormed off, frustrated. This is bull shit; I can't even add my own boyfriend to my phone. I'm going to have to do something more, I just have to figure out exactly what. As I cleaned up my face and hands, I stared around my room, it was a disaster. I couldn't even see the floors, because of the filthy dirty laundry all over them, mixed in with piles of trash from junk food I've smuggled in from school. My parents gave me my very own washer and dryer, so I could stay on top of my laundry, I just refused to do it. Laundry was beneath me. I chuckled, because I knew when I left one day, I was not going to be the one straightening up my room. I'd take my necessities, and then make like a donkey-dick and hit the road. I knew my parents wouldn't be the one cleaning it, they'd likely hire some maid or cleaning lady to come and do it for them. I thought about the piles of soiled underwear and half eaten midnight snacks. One day, I'd have to have a man who would make enough money to hire a cleaning lady every day, because I wasn't about to be the one doing it.

The next day at school, I told Zeb that I told my parents about us. "Really, Ursella flat out said she didn't give a crap, that she didn't trust me enough to talk to anyone, let alone a boy."

"Hmm, she really does have a tight leash on you, I'm really sorry."

"It's okay, I'll make it," I said with gusto.

Zeb smiled at me softly. "You look very pretty today. One day, I will be able to take you on dates. As my dad said, I need to make sure I'm taking you on dates, as often as I'm able. When we are able to go on a date, what do you want to do? Would you like to go bowling with me?"

I smiled. "I'd go bowling with you, but I don't think I'd actually bowl. I wouldn't mind hanging out and cheering you on while you bowled. Bowling just isn't my thing. I just cannot wait until we are able to be a little more free."

At lunch that same day, Zeb had already gone to work, and I was sitting with Sadie.

"What are you going to do since your parents won't let you add Zeb to your phone, which likely means they won't let you go on dates with him either? How are you going to keep your relationship alive and well?"

I giggled. "Girl, I don't need to be able to go on dates with Zeb to keep my relationship with him alive and well. He is truly smitten with me. I mean, why wouldn't he be? Besides that, I have less than a year until I'm eighteen. I have some ideas going through my head, that may pan out. Did you know that his parents don't give him a bedtime or a curfew? They ask him to do a couple of simple chores around the house, and that's about it."

"I didn't know that. I think it's probably because he's very trustworthy… or maybe they just don't think he has it in him to do anything… that, you know, you would do," she said with a laugh.

"Maybe… just maybe. It does get me thinking though."

"About what?"

"Well, I'm just thinking about what it would be like to live with Zeb. I'm curious how it would feel to have that much freedom and no oversight."

"Yeah, I can see how that could be appealing to someone who's in your position, but as someone who has all that as well, I can tell you that it's not all that it's cut out to be. I go to school, go home, and repeat. Occasionally, I will babysit for someone, and earn a little money, but in reality, it just feels a little lonely." Sadie stared off into the distance thoughtfully, then smiled. "It is nice though, to not have to ask to go do things. I just let my mom know that I'm going to be going to a dance, and she says 'have fun! Do you need money?'"

I looked at Sadie for a moment, really looked at her. She was pretty, short, thin, with dark hair down to the middle of her back. She wore glasses and had light skin, with an occasional pimple deftly hidden with foundation on her forehead. She was very bookish. She had pretty white teeth, a slight over-bight on her k-9 teeth. She always smelled like one of those fancy perfumes my parents are always buying me. I realized right then that I hated the way she looked.

"Girl, you should let me do your makeup sometime,

it would be fun to have a little make-over party and hang," I said sweetly. "You could come over, and we could sit around and use that big, magnified mirror my mom got me for my birthday. It would be really fun!"

I knew that she would never be coming over, I'd never actually follow through with one of the dates we planned for it. Besides, after tonight, if all went to plan, I wouldn't have to worry about my mom and dad anymore, at all.

I got home from school, knowing no one would be there and I began by setting into motion the plans I had made. It would start with not taking my dog out and letting him go potty on the floor. Come to think of it, if I didn't have an automatic dog feeder, he would likely have starved. I always forget about little things like that. I knew if my mom got home, and saw some dog mess on the floor, she would lose her mind, especially two days in a row.

My mom yelled, "What is this!? Tanna, did you not see the poop on the floor of the kitchen!? Get your butt in here and clean this up!"

I ignored my mom at first, because I knew it would make her even more mad. After a few moments I yelled out through the house, "I'm busy, you clean it up!" From there the fight ensued. My mom and I went back and forth, and I kept pushing her until finally she had had enough.

She was red in the face and sweating a lot. Tears of fury brimmed into her eyes, and she huffed quickly. My mom isn't a big lady, she isn't very tall, but she has a few years on her. She aged fairly well, being fifteen years younger than my dad, he was in his sixties, and she was in her fifties.

She fumed, "I just cannot wait until you are no longer living here! I truly just cannot wait!"

"Oh, you want me to leave!?" I screamed back.

"I wish you would," she fumed.

"Fine! I'm leaving! I'm going to call someone now!"

I grabbed my phone and hit enter on the number I had pre-dialed into my phone, before I started the fight. It rang three times and then his voice came across the line, sweet and kind, and full of concern.

"Hello? Tanna?"

I started crying and sniffling, putting on a show, "My mom and dad are kicking me out. I have nowhere to go. I don't know what to do."

"Hold on one second, let me talk to my parents."

I heard a shuffling and scuffling sound, followed by a door opening, and shutting loudly. A moment later, I heard another door open, and the random mutterings of a television playing in the background.

"Dad! Tanna's parents kicked her out," Zeb said quickly.

A second man's voice responded, "Well go get her, we will figure it out in the morning."

A woman's voice responded, "Oh my god! Are you serious? She's seventeen! Go get her!"

"What's your address?"

"31 Blueberry Lane, big house, on top of the hill, you can't miss it."

"I'll be there in a few minutes Tanna."

"Okay, thank you." I smiled; my plan was working perfectly. I am going to tell them that I got locked out by the worst parents the world has ever seen. I knew what I wanted, and I knew exactly how to get it.

Part 3

Chapter 7
Sanctuary?

By the time Zeb got to my parents' house, I was practically floating with glee. Gloating if you will, towards my parents who were absolutely furious. It's funny, looking back now, how little I cared that my parents were so upset with my behavior. What did they expect? They taught me to go after exactly what I wanted, and to have the determination to do whatever it took to get it. Afterall, I am just a product of them. If anything, it's their fault for what happened.

I was on several different types of medication, one for psychosis, one for anxiety, one for birth-control, and one for mood-stabilization. I had decided a few days before that I was not going to be taking any more of my medications. I didn't need them, so to hell with them, I'd bring them with me, because I was certain that I could weaponize that information at some point. It was also a plus that taking the anxiety pill had a way of making me not care about anything, and I really did enjoy that feeling.

I had one large trash bag full of a small portion of my clothes, really—only the clean clothes. The dirty ones will be left behind, so that some poor housekeeper can clean it up. I also left behind my needy little dog. I didn't want my new hosts to see how I felt about that dog. I would have to keep things on the downlow so that they will grow to trust me and give me the same freedom Zeb got.

Zeb pulled up to my house in a silver Chevy SUV. I was standing on the porch, and quickly started the waterworks up, so that he would see just how devastated I was, or at least make him think I was devastated. When he hopped out, he rushed over to me and quickly wrapped me in a tight hug, I felt like he would save me from the world, if only I would let him.

He whispered gently into the night, "It's going to be okay Tanna. We will figure it all out, I promise."

I smiled into his chest, he couldn't see my face, so I made a sniffling sound, and said, "I don't know how it could be okay, but thank you for being here for me."

After a quick glance at the porch, Zeb let me go and walked towards the over-sized large trash bag I had left, like so much garbage. He grabbed the bag, hefted it easily, and walked back towards the vehicle, opened the back hatch, and sat it gently inside. After closing the hatch, Zeb glanced at me, smiled sweetly, and held his hand out for me to take.

"Come on, let's go home."

Zeb walked me around to the passenger side door and opened it for me. Of course, he did, a gentleman through and through. Without a backwards glance, he pulled out of my parent's driveway and headed across town, towards the downtown hospital. I vaguely remember him telling me about how he lived near or next to the hospital and could sometimes hear the med-flight helicopter landing and taking off in the middle of the night. It wasn't very far from my parent's house, but it was far enough that I felt like I had a little more breathing room to work my magic and be out from under the stresses and controlling thumbs of those hateful people.

Pulling into the driveway, I couldn't notice much of the outside of the building, because of how dark it was on this moonless night. I could see a little with the solar lamps that sporadically decorated the front yard, shining light on a medium sized brick home. Standing in the front door, behind a glass storm door, was a man and a woman, I assumed were the same ones I had heard on the phone when I called Zeb. We parked outside a garage door and got out. Zeb quickly grabbed my bag, and came around to hold my hand, as we walked under the porch awning.

As we walked through his front door, the first thing I noticed was Christmas. It was Christmas everything in his house. The living room was far longer than it was wide, and it was decorated to the teeth. A beautiful Christmas tree was on full display, with all the branches covered in snow flecking. There were red berries, and small woodland critter creatures poking out of the branches. A large barn-owl was sitting on the crown of the tree, where most people would put a star. Lining the left and right walls of the first twenty feet of the living room, were bookshelves. On the top of each of the shelves were various Santa Claus dolls, and a few reindeer in between. There was garland on a coat rack directly to my right, as we walked in, and lit up, twinkling garland that was strung on the shelves. The rugs that sat upon the grey wood grained hardwood floors were a bright cheery Christmas red. The throw pillows on a large white sectional were all of Christmas orientation. Little did I know at the time, that this Christmas display would grow on my heart, and become a place that I would look back fondly on for the rest of my life. Any time anyone would talk about Christmas decorations, this was the example that floated through my mind.

"Hi, I'm Parker, I'm Zeb's dad, nice to meet you." He reached out and shook my hand. "I'm sorry you're having to go through this, our home is yours for as long as you choose to stay here."

He was tall, like Zeb, but a lot more weight around his bones than Zeb had. The epitome of a dad bod, it was easy to see that he carried most of his extra weight around his midriff, likely from drinking his share of beer. He had short, dark brown hair, and reddish colored facial hair, which he had in sort of an unkempt goatee.

A woman, a little taller than me, rushed towards me and wrapped me in a hug. She had brown hair and bright green eyes. Her perfect teeth, really stuck out in my mind when I thought of her. She was super sweet, and kind. I came to learn that Zeb's family often referred to her as, 'Mother Christmas' because of her extraordinary decorations.

"Oh you poor thing! Don't you worry, you are welcome here. I'm Clementine, but everyone calls me Clemmy, this is our home. Zeb! Get her some blankets and a pillow for the couch, we will figure out better sleeping arrangements in the morning." Clemmy let me go, barking orders around the house. "Come with me hon, I will show you where everything is."

"This is our kitchen, you're welcome to anything we have." She walked me through the living room towards a large opening in the wall, a sliding barn-door entryway. I saw a clean kitchen, with a snack-bar setup on the counter. "This is the hot-cocoa bar. There're pastries, brownies, and anything you could need to make a good hot cocoa. If you're hungry now, I can make you something to eat."

"I'm not hungry, thank you."

"Okay, it's no problem," she said, with a knowing look on her face.

"I bet you're not, after going through what you went through tonight," Parker said, "just know that the stuff is here, if you do get an appetite."

Clemmy continued the tour by showing me where the pantry was, which was fully stocked and loaded with snacks, canned goods, and anything someone may need to make biscuits. Afterwards, she showed me where the spare bathroom was, through a laundry-room that was turned into an office/laundry room combination.

"This is where I work, when I'm working from home, and this is the little bathroom. I only ask that you use one of the other bathrooms, if you see this door closed and I'm working from home, because I may be in a meeting."

"Okay," I said tentatively, sweet, and docile.

About then, three orange cats darted out of a small cat door that was installed into the garage door, that separated the garage from the rest of the house. I came to learn that the fat cat's name was Archibald Winston, the tall cat's name was Zukovi Alexander, and the smallest cat's name was Stanely Fitzgerald. I do recall them being the funniest and most loving cat trio I've ever seen.

"Archibald is my cat," Parker said, as he stooped and picked up the fat mewling cat. "He's a fat boy, but definitely the most playful and people friendly cat we have. The other two are friendly too, they just don't know immediately if someone is going to be able to pet them or not. That tall butterscotch cat, which Clemmy calls her butterscotch baby, is Clemmy's baby, Zukovi, but we just call him Zuko. That one right there, that sweet little boy is Stanley. He's one hundred percent Zeb's cat. That cat lives and breathes for Zeb, he even follows him around, or meows at him to have Zeb follow him, to show him where he likes to play. Which is in the garage."

About that time, Zeb walked back into the living room with a bundle of blankets and a pillow, that he set gently on the couch. Parker and Clemmy went down a hallway towards what I assumed was their bedroom. Zeb sat down on the couch and smiled at me.

"Come, sit down next to me." He lightly patted the couch at his right side and smiled.

"Why are your parents so nice?" I asked.

"They just are, they got their faults, but they are really nice people."

I didn't have much else to say, so I just leaned into him, and started to cry. I wanted him to think I was completely heartbroken over what happened that night. I needed him to perceive me as a meek and mild little girl, who couldn't take care of herself.

I lay there until I fell asleep leaning next to him. At some point, he got up, covered me more completely with a blanket and set a pillow by my head. He then went to his own bedroom and went to bed. I awoke with a small start when his bedroom door shut. Not one time did he try to grope me, or kiss me, or anything. 'Always the gentleman,' I thought with disgust as I drifted off to sleep again.

The next morning, I woke up to the smell of bacon, eggs, and the soft rattle of pots, pans, and dishes. It smelled amazing. I sat up on the couch, but I didn't move, it was still a new environment, so I was a little nervous about the normal everyday routines people had. I didn't want to over-step my bounds yet and ruin this opportunity I was given.

"You hungry?" Parker asked me, poking his head around the corner of the kitchen.

"Not really," I lied, knowing that it was probably what would be expected for someone going through a 'traumatic' situation.

"Well, if there's anything you need, Clemmy will be up soon, and we will get a list together, and head to the store afterwhile. This is just to make sure you're well taken care of."

"Thank you."

Around twenty minutes later, Clemmy got up smiled at me and then walked into the kitchen, she hugged and kissed Parker, and commented on the food he was cooking.

"Mmmmmm, that smells delicious. Are you going to make some toast for me too? You know how much I like toast!"

He laughed. "I made biscuits and gravy, I'm not making any damn toast."

"Fiiiine, I'll eat the biscuits and gravy," she said, acting like she was pouting. It was really cute, seeing old people act this way. "I'm going to go talk to Tanna about what we discussed last night, come join us when you are finished here."

"Ok babe, I'm about done now, so I'll come with

you."

A moment later, both Parker, Clemmy, and I were sitting on the couch, discussing the current situation. It was blowing my mind at just how trusting and giving these people were. I would never trust some random teenager that wanted to come stay at my house, especially my son's girlfriend.

"So, we discussed this last night, after we went to bed. As a mandatory reporter, I have to report the situation that we have here. I have to report that your parents locked you out of your home and were not allowing you to live there anymore. If I don't report it, we could potentially face some legal challenges, or potentially cost me my job. No one wants anything like that happening, so we will check all our boxes and cross all of our t's," Clemmy explained, being mindful of the sensitive topic. "Tell us what happened."

"So, I got into an argument with my mom and dad, about stupid stuff. My mom yelled at me to get out of her house, and my dad screamed, 'get the f. out, and don't come back!' It was really scary," I lied.

"Zeb told us that you were adopted. How could someone do something like that to a child who has gone through so much in her young life? Really, how could someone do that to a child period, let alone a child that they had adopted!?" Clemmy gasped.

"So, here's the deal Tanna, Clemmy and I discussed this, and we decided you will be allowed to stay here as long as you want. We will turn the den into a bedroom for you, I just only have one rule. My one rule is that you will go to school. I don't care if you don't get a job, I don't care if you don't do extra-curricular stuff after school. I just want you going to school and focusing all your attention on your grades. Do you have plans on your education after you graduate? You're in the 11th grade, right?"

"Yes, I'm in the 11th grade. I do have a job; I work over at the Green Chicken. It's just one or two days a week, but I do work."

"Ooh they have pretty good salads over there," Clemmy said.

"Ok, so go to school every day, work if you want, if you don't, then don't. That's my requirement, do you have any issues with that?" said Parker.

"Of course not. I love going to school."

"Also, you should note that you and Zeb do not have to be in a relationship together for you to live here. If either of you decide that you're better off not being in one, then that's okay, you're not going to be kicked out because of it. We will not be kicking you out of the house unless you're getting arrested for doing something crazy." Clemmy laughed.

Zeb got up a few minutes later, and his dad pulled him aside, to let him know the same things that Clemmy and I were just discussing. It was nice to see that his parents were so caring and were focused on making sure the home was healthy and happy.

Zeb's little brother got up from bed, wandered into the kitchen and sat down to eat some breakfast. He didn't acknowledge or even register that anyone else was in the living room that he just passed through. Parker laughed and got up to make sure he got all the food he wanted for breakfast.

"That's Des, he's 10. He probably stayed up too late playing on his phone without permission, that's why he's acting like a zombie right now," Clemmy explained. "Don't worry, he's a goofball, you'll love him."

I smiled, thinking that things were going to be going very smoothly from here on out. I am certain this would be my sanctuary. Things were definitely looking up, and very soon, I would have the trust and freedom that Zeb had from these very gullible and easily fooled old people. I still had work to do to get exactly what I wanted, but I knew how to do it, and I would get it done.

Chapter 8
My Emotions

"**I** don't have any bras, or a toothbrush, or socks. I'm sorry, I probably left them all at my parents' house." I was telling Clemmy about some of the items I needed. "I'd really like some makeup too, I don't know much about how to put my own makeup on, as my parents wouldn't let me put them on. Do you think you can teach me how?"

"That's okay! We will take you to get everything you may need, and of course I will teach you how." She looked at Parker and grinned, "We will just take Mr. grumpy-pants' bank card and go shopping."

He rolled his eyes and mumbled something incoherently. It was nice having what seemed like a normal interaction of a family. We were all sitting around the living room, on the big white sectional sofa, talking about how things were going to be going, and what was needed. My phone dinged in my pocket, since getting here, I had turned off location, but my phone was still under parental supervision and regulation. I'd have to figure out how to get that taken care of, so that I could use my phone any way I wanted.

Mom: Tanna, you need to come clean out this bedroom. Your father and I will not be here today, so it needs to be taken care of today. Everything needs to be removed from this room.

Mom: It's unacceptable that someone else should have to clean up this incredible mess. You need to be here today to take care of this room.

I frowned and then told Clemmy and Parker, "My mom is telling me I need to come clean out the room. She wants me to remove everything in the room."

"Everything? Like… all the furniture and bedding? I am not sure where we would be able to put all of that, or any of that for that matter." Clemmy frowned.

"Yeah, that's not going to happen. You and Zeb should go over there and get all the little things you're missing, make sure you bring back anything you're wanting to keep," Parker offered.

"Okay, we can do that. My parents were so abusive, my mom was always putting me down and calling me names, and my dad was always drinking. Every single day, he was drinking like four or five beers," I explained.

"I don't think four or five beers is a terrible amount of beer. Not saying it's a good thing, I just know folks who are drinking a thirty pack a day," Parker said.

"Well, he would drink those tiny little vodka bottles, the little one-shot bottles as well. He'd be drinking a few of those each night too, then he'd sit around and just ignore me." I added quickly, "The smell of alcohol really triggers my trauma. The guy who used to rape me, his breath would smell like beer, he knew that, and still kept drinking, even though I told him it bothered me."

"I understand. Well, we don't drink very often, but when we plan on it, we will make sure you have a safe space to be, so that you're not put in an uncomfortable position," Clemmy said encouragingly.

"Yeah, I can definitely see how that would cause you some mental stress, I'm sorry you had to go through all that."

Internally, I smiled. I knew that this was going very well, and I would go over to my old house and get some of the things I wanted from there, like my cd's and some of my nicer clothes, and a couple of my stuffed animals. I still would not clean up anything, it would be a win-win.

Zeb came and gave me a hug, while carrying his lunch box and wearing his leather jacket. He was about to head to work. As he was a hardworking man, it was hard for me not to admire his work ethic and dedication to his job. He can go out and earn some money, and then spoil me with it.

"Bye Tanna, I'll see you this evening."

"Bye Zeb!"

Around thirty minutes later, Clemmy and I went to the store and picked up some of the necessities that a seventeen-year-old girl would need. We grabbed me a new toothbrush, some bras and underwear, and several types of make-up. We even grabbed some cute press-on nails. It was almost thanksgiving, so Clemmy and I wanted to be a little more festive for the holiday season. I'd never used press on nails, and my mom wouldn't let me get my nails done at the nail salon, because I didn't take care of them. I liked to chew my nails and pick at them, until they fell off. My mom decided that it was just too wasteful.

After we got back to the house, we came bouncing up the driveway, and skipped on into the house carrying our stuff from the store. Parker had taken the other vehicle and went to the hardware store while we were out. He wanted to buy some curtain rails to install between the den and the dining room, so that I could have a wall, and a little bit of privacy. The curtain was large, and a Christmas red that seemed to brighten up the area with a festive cheer. It went from the ceiling to the floor, without a gap between. It wasn't too heavy that the cats weren't able to push their way through, in order to get to that half of the house and the garage. I had access to my own bathroom, and the garage, which had an outside door that always stayed locked. I felt safe, because Parker and Clemmy kept cameras pointed at all of their doors, can't ever tell how the neighborhood watch works anymore. Sometimes they are awesome, and sometimes they don't work at all. Parker and Des had moved a small one-person bed into the den and made the bed up with sheets, blankets, and pillows. It was located next to some in-the-wall permanently mounted bookshelves that were loaded down heavily with books of all types. Most of the books were adventure and fantasy books, but some of them were of the more, smut-filled style, that I preferred. There were a few educational books, but most of those were on the bookshelves that lined the living room walls. I had my own television mounted up on the wall. There was a small cabinet under the television that had some old unopen bottles of whiskey, and a small wine rack in it. They were pushed back towards the back end of the cabinet and had some boxes of Christmas figurines that didn't make the decorative cut this year, set in front of them. I only found them because I was digging through the cabinets one night, a couple weeks later. All in all, I was very satisfied with my new set up, it's not as glamorous as my old home, or my old room, but it was definitely sufficient, especially if I garnered the same freedom and perks that Zeb was graced with.

"Ooh this looks good! That's such a nice curtain, we can definitely change the curtain color too after the holiday season, so that it's not always Christmas colors," Clemmy exclaimed.

"After the holiday season? You mean after Valentine's Day?" Parker joked.

"Of course," Clemmy said with all the sincerity in the world.

"Fine, but you're picking the color and buying the next curtain. It needs to be 192 inches long, and 108 inches tall."

"Okay. I can do that."

Clemmy worked for the state, as the Director of one of the many departments. Parker worked as a maintenance man at one of the factories local to the city. They weren't the wealthiest of people, but they weren't doing poorly either, they were solidly in the middle class.

"Do you want to see what we got at the store?" Clemmy asked.

"Sure, let me get these last couple of fasteners screwed in for this rail and I'll be right there," he said while climbing up a three-step step stool.

A couple moments later, I started pulling out some of the makeup and smaller items I got from the store. "I got this palette, and this eyeliner to go with it. It's going to look so cute!" I said, holding up the palette and eyeliner.

"Very nice makeup."

"I also got this bag of peppermint bark chocolate,

it's my favorite."

"That looks good, I don't think I've tried that, I bet it would be good mixed into hot cocoa," Parker said.

"We also both got some of these adorable Christmas nails! Look at the little reindeer and Santa on them!" I practically screamed with glee.

"Hmm, what did that cost?" Parker asked Clemmy, who was standing there with a big grin on her face.

"We saved 129$ with our purchase!" I said before Clemmy got a chance to answer.

"How much did ya'll spend?" Parker asked again.

"We saved like 40% of our purchase, we spent a little over 225$," Clemmy said with a chuckle. "Like Tanna said, we saved 129$."

"You didn't save anything, you spent 250$. That's not saving anything. Damn girl math. That's not how that works," Parker said with an amused look on his face.

"Well, we totally saved because we were definitely going to be buying this stuff, so we could have spent a lot more," I said as a matter of fact.

Parker grumbled and then walked out of the dining room. I quickly went to put away the new items I got from the store, and then sat down in the den, which now became my bedroom. It was nice, I had a big window that overlooked the backyard. The view of the backyard was essentially just a small dying garden that was mounted to the side of an off-white shed, and then the hospital. It really was close; I felt I could likely stand at the back door and spit on the hospital wall. Well, that's a small exaggeration, but I could definitely hit it with a rock.

DING

-Mom: Well? Are you going to be coming to get your stuff today? I haven't heard back from you.

-Me: Yes, I'll come get some of my things, I don't know where I'm going to put all the furniture, so I'm not getting that.

-Mom: Something needs to be done with all that stuff.

-Me: Yes. What's going to happen with my car? I would also like to be able to add who I want to my phone contact list, can you please unlock the parental locks.

-Mom: Your car will be put in the shop tomorrow; you can go pick it up next week when it's done. Don't worry, you won't have to pay anything, it's all covered. They said they won't charge us because they are friends of the family.

-Me: Okay. And my phone?

-Mom: The password is: #1031Daughter

I rolled my eyes at the password. I bet she changed it to my birthday and 'Daughter' because she knew I'd be asking for the password. At least now I can control my own phone. Time to download my group messaging apps and snaps, and other apps to communicate with people. This is going to be great!

-Me: Thanks. Zeb and I will be by to grab some more of my things this afternoon around 5:30 pm.

-Mom: Okay. We won't be there. Please lock up after you're done.

-Me: Will do.

A couple of hours later, Zeb came home from work. I met him at the door, I was dressed in a cute little pink hat, a rumpled t-shirt, and a small skirt. I liked to look good. Clemmy and I had the same sized foot, so she very kindly let me borrow some knee-high boots to complete my outfit. I looked phenomenal.

"Wow! You look stunning," Zeb said, looking me up and down. "I really like that outfit."

"Aww you really like my 'fit? You're so sweet, thank you so much. May I hug you?" I said sweetly.

"Of course." He put his arms out and pulled me into a warm tight embrace.

"We have to go to my parents' house today to get some more of my things. My mom demanded that I did that today. She's such a jerk! It's really bothering me that she's texting me so much."

I really poured it on thick, in truth, my mom wasn't saying anything that was upsetting, she seemed like she was actually being very cordial. I just didn't want to put her in a good light to anyone. She was an old school style parent, rules with an iron fist, except she never hit me. State law for adoption would never tolerate any sort of physical abuse. I spent most of my time egging her on, nagging and pushing her buttons until she started yelling at me, and then I acted like a victim. Doing this made it so easy to garner affection and empathy from others.

"Don't worry Tanna, you're safe from that environment now. I will do everything I can to never allow anyone to hurt you again," Zeb said, as he continued to hold me.

Upon arriving at my parent's home, I told Zeb just to wait for me in the car. I didn't want him to see my room, or even getting a whiff of how nasty I left things for whoever ended up cleaning it up. My dog was here, staring and barking at the door, tail wagging like a buffoon. Hank was probably incredibly happy to see me. As I walked through the door, I nudged him aside with my muddied shoe.

"Get off me stupid dog."

I grabbed a couple of large trash bags from my dad's attached shop and went to my old room. I piled in some of my sluttier dirty clothes, and a big hoodie that I took from Kyle. I wasn't about to lose this one. I snatched up some of my jewelry, a couple large bags of stuffed animals, and a couple of my electronics that I may want to use at some point. All in all, there wasn't much else I wanted in my old room. Standing in the doorway, I laughed because I still couldn't see my floor. The smell alone of that room was stale, and smelled like soured milk combined with a wound that was just on the verge of going septic. This was the perfect way I wanted to leave my room to my parents, trashed and rotten. Just what they deserved.

After Zeb and I piled the bags into the car, I figured I would need to progress our relationship a little bit. It would be easy to upgrade my small den room into his bedroom. I just had to give him a little bit of the sugar, I so willingly shared with others.

"Want to see a little spot I like to go to, to think sometimes?" I asked innocently.

"Sure, where are we headed?"

"Just take a left here, go about a half mile, and there's a little dirt road on the right that goes down to a small boat ramp at a creek."

"Okay."

He seemed completely oblivious. It was cute really, him being an eighteen-year-old boy, being so naïve and innocent. It just made this type of thing that much easier. We pulled up to the small, rounded dirt and gravel lot that sat atop an old boat ramp, that led down to a slowly ebbing creek.

"I would walk down here sometimes, and just sit over there, next to that Game and Fish sign. It's so quiet and peaceful, not a lot of people come down here. Come on, hop out with me, let's walk down to the water."

We got out of the car and wandered down towards the water. He didn't reach for my hand or try to walk super close to me. In fact, he had a goofy smile on his face, because he felt the unerring call for adventure. The call for adventure that comes from exploring somewhere he'd never been. He stared off at the water, flowing slowly in the fading light of the day, showing pure excitement on his face. I could tell that he loved being outdoors.

"Have you ever fished down here? Do you even like fishing?" he asked softly, not wanting to disturb the evening peace and quiet.

"I haven't, but my dad has, he's caught some good-sized small mouth bass in here, or maybe it was crappie. I don't remember. I do like to fish, I just don't get to go that often, because every time my dad goes, he goes without inviting me."

"I'll take you fishing, my dad and I go fishing all the time. We love it. You can even come out in the kayaks and fish with us. It's such a great time."

"Kayaks?"

"Yeah! We have six out back behind the little shed."

"That would be nice…" I trailed off as I stepped closer to him, standing in front of him. I looked up at his face, and he looked down into my eyes. We held each other's gaze for a few silent seconds. It was almost as if the creek came to a sudden halt, the birds held their breaths, and the rest of the world faded into nothing. I reached up, put my hands around the back of his head, and pulled his face gently towards mine. We shared a kiss that lasted what seemed like hours. He wasn't aggressive, more tentative and testing. It was the kiss of a boy getting his first kiss, but it wasn't mine. As easily as I guided him, he learned. It was the first time I really felt like I was teaching someone who was eager to learn, but not so eager that he let his hands stray, or his aggression take over. He was the gentlest person I have ever kissed. For the first time in my life, I began to second guess my decision to use Zeb for my gain. I set my resolve, knowing what I wanted. It would just be a little more difficult to get it, now that I let my emotions get involved.

Chapter 9
Watch My Step

The next morning, I awoke and was greeted with a deep groan of thunder from the clouds in the sky, bellies full of rain and lightning. They rolled to the east quickly, beating and strumming sheets of rain, in a roar, occasionally a flash and crack of lightning breaking the tempo. I arose and got dressed in some of my everyday clothing. Zeb was going to be driving me to school today in Clemmy's car. If it was a nice day, and Zeb wasn't able to take me to school, I would either be walking, or taking my own car, if I ever got it out of the shop. I still needed to tell Parker and Clemmy about that.

Zeb stuck his head around the open bathroom door and shot me a quick greeting and question, "Good morning, Tanna, are you about ready to go?"

Nodding I said, "Yup. I got everything I need."

I went out to the car and climbed in, he shut and made sure the house door locked before following me to the car. It was warm inside the car; Zeb had gotten up a little earlier and started it up. I looked over at him, and leaned towards him when he climbed in. He took the lean as a request for a kiss and gave me a small peck on my lips before strapping on his seatbelt and backing out of the driveway.

"I think my dad will be able to pick you up from

school today, since I have work. He said he'd meet you by the exit of the school by Juan Pepe's to take you home."

"That will be nice, I'd hate to have to walk home in this weather."

"Yeah, that would be terrible."

I was sitting in geometry next to Sadie, learning about isolating acute triangles. Sadie knew that I had been 'kicked out' of my parent's house and was now living with Zeb. I also told her about me finally getting to have my phone unlocked. It was very satisfying being able to text, call, or add anyone I wanted into my phone.

"So, you and Zeb do it yet? I know y'all are living together now."

I laughed. "No, but we did kiss yesterday. Let me tell you girl, it was really nice. I think I was his first kiss though, we haven't spoken much about it, but I feel like I was. It wasn't sloppy like most people's first kisses are, but it definitely felt awkward."

"Hmm, I've never seen him with anyone else, hell I've never seen him even talking to anyone else, so you may be right."

The teacher glared at us for talking in class while he was trying to teach. We didn't care, there were so many kids in this school, that the teachers just pretty much ignored us, if we failed, we failed. My grades were terrible, I was borderline failing half my classes anyway. I wasn't dumb, I just refused to do my homework. I'd marry a man with money one day, anyway.

"Well, what are your plans this weekend? It's going to be nice outside, maybe some really romantic walks, or parking your car somewhere?" Sadie teased.

"I don't know, we may just hang out at the house, I think his parents are going on a date Friday night, I don't know how long their dates usually last, but I may be able to get some alone time with Zeb then."

At ten after three that day, Parker was where he said he'd be, and I didn't have to walk back home. It wasn't far, only about three quarters of a mile away, but still, I was chubby and I did not like walking that far. It was a relatively quiet ride back to the house, except for a few customary questions about how my day was, and if I was feeling alright from Parker.

I went and lay down in Zeb's room on his bed, he wasn't going to be getting home until around 4:30 pm. Parker didn't care, he was busy trying to play some War game on a game system. That's how his brothers and sisters and him hung out. Sometimes in person, but usually they just played a couple rounds of the game and then hopped off and went to take care of their responsibilities.

Lying there, I opened up my group messaging app, and started scrolling through the support group. A long time ago, I had started a support group that, on the face of it, was to help young people who were feeling down in the dumps and going through some mental struggles. These were the kind of people that I knew how to manipulate and get them to do anything I wanted. Most every member of my "support group" on this messaging app was a boy between the ages of twelve and seventeen. I liked to target them because they were already vulnerable, and I was easily able to relate to them. They felt an increased confidence with it being online, that they could shower me with all sorts of attention. I haven't been on this app in almost a year because of my mom. She found out and locked my phone down, I had just started getting some privileges back when the Virginia incident occurred.

The second I logged back into my account; I saw the forty or fifty different people that had messaged me. I sent a basic follow up message to all of them, seeing who all was still on this app.

-Me: Hey babes, sorry I haven't been around, my mom locked my phone down like it was Fort Knox. I just now got it back; I missed you so much.

I just copied and sent that to every single person. It didn't matter who all was on the app, it's not like they communicated with each other, and they were from all over the United States. I didn't expect too many hits, after all, it had been nearly a year. I could always send my feelers back out and try to get more people to join the group. It isn't hard, social media makes everything easy. The first reply didn't take long, it was from an old friend named Lucky.

-Lucky: Hey! Where have you been!? I've been worried sick about you. You haven't been around for almost a year. I think about you all the time.

-Me: Hey Lucky! Yeah sorry, my Nazi of a mom had complete lockdown on everything I had. I couldn't get a message out to anyone.

-Lucky: Dang that's nuts! I totally get it. So, what have you been up to?

-Me: Oh this and that. Not a lot really, going to school, working a little. What about you?

-Lucky: Oh! I got this new Star machine block set, that I've been putting a lot of time into. It is truly massive, like 2500 pieces. There is literally an entire

200-page book of directions. It's going to be a replica of a big ship capable of killing an entire planet. Other than that, I've been good. Not too many bad days, occasionally, but for the most part not a lot.

-Me: That's good to hear, I bet that big block set would be super fun to put together. I'd love to help you with that sometime, if only I was able to get to South Carolina.

-Lucky: Yeah, I wish that too. Hey, can I ask you something? I'm a little nervous. It's been so long; I just don't know how to ask you.

-Me: Yes! You can ask me anything.

-Lucky: Are you still my girlfriend? I really do love you.

-Me: Of course I'm still your girlfriend. You're my Lucky Charms. Let's face time, is it still the same number?

-Lucky: Okay phew, and yes, it's the same number.

Lucky's face popped up on my phone's screen a few moments later. He was young and thin, with a little bit of facial hair on his cheeks. He was fifteen years old, but he looked like he was my age. He had mahogany brown hair, and deep brown eyes. Those eyes always shined super bright when he saw me, it was just pure adulation about how I looked.

"Wow, you look so good. You are so beautiful. I wish I could just kiss your face right now. I wish I could hold your body and touch you all over," Lucky said.

"Aww me too! I really could use that. I do want to tell you something, so I am living with a new family right now. That being said when I face time you, I can't speak to you like I'm your girlfriend, because they'll get mad and kick me out. I had to get away from my parents, they had me really locked down. Is that okay?"

"I totally get that. It's definitely okay."

"Awesome! I'll face time you every single day then. I can even call you at night sometime, and we can have a little more privacy." I smiled really big, hinting at secret nighttime occurrences.

We talked for about forty-five minutes, and when I noticed the time, it was close to four-thirty. "I am going to get off here and get ready to have some dinner. I love you Lucky Charms. I'll talk to you later."

"I love you too Tanna!"

After hanging up the phone, I hopped out of the bed and walked out into the living room and sat down on the couch. I kept scrolling through my phone watching the little videos on the vine app. Most of them were smut-like videos that I skipped through really quick, some were funny ones that I watched. If I did this enough, it would change my algorithm, and I would get primarily funny videos. I smiled as I thought, 'I could manipulate anything.'

After dinner that night, Zeb, Parker, Clemmy, and myself were sitting on the couch just talking about stuff. I remembered my car, and thought it was a perfect time to bring it up.

"My car is in the shop; I can pick it up in a few days. It shouldn't cost anything because the shop people know my parents, and they said they were friends, and our money was no good there."

"Oh, what kind of car do you have?" Parker asked.

"I got a Toyota Corolla. It's not much, but I love my car. It's in the shop because someone came down the parking lot aisle too fast and rear-ended me. I wasn't even in my car, it was parked. It was the craziest thing."

"That's wild! Where did that happen at?" Clemmy asked with wide eyes.

"We were over at O'Shally's setting up an appointment for my birthday party, which turned out to be a bust, but still."

"Dang, that's rough. What happened at your birthday party that made it a bust? I haven't been over to O'Shally's yet, but I hear it is big and nice," Parker said.

Zeb was just sitting there, smiling at the conversation, not putting any input in of his own. He was just happy, sitting in his own private happy town. I thought it was super cute that he was smiling and not saying anything.

"Well, for one thing my ex-boyfriend showed up without being invited. That made it super uncomfortable."

"How did he know where your birthday party was?" Parker asked, looking at me quizzically.

"Well, he had text me earlier that day, and told me happy birthday, then asked me what we were doing for my birthday. I told him we were going to O'Shally's. He said, 'Bet, I'll be right there.' Honestly, it was all super weird and uncomfortable."

For the first time, I recognized that Parker had a similar look in his eyes that my mother got when she knew I was lying. It was like he could see right through my words, to the truth. His reddish beard rose a little as he pursed his lips in thought. I realized he was thinking about how to say something, without it being completely rude.

"Let me ask you a question Tanna," he said very calmly. "How come your ex-boyfriend's phone number was even in your phone? You made it very clear to Zeb that you weren't allowed to date or have anyone else's phone number in your phone because your mom kept you on lock-down."

Hesitantly, I said, "Well, my mom and dad let me have him in my phone because he 'was a good sort,' and his family was friends of theirs."

"Why did you keep him in your phone after you two broke up?"

"Well, he sometimes gets in a really dark place, and needs to talk about it. So, he calls me, and I help him out. It's why I lead support groups, to help my friends out if they get into a really dark place and want to hurt themselves." The lies flowed smoothly out of my mouth. I messed up when I told them about Kyle coming to my birthday party. I shouldn't have done that.

"Listen, I'm going to be blunt here Tanna. I don't give a rat's ass about those other kids, I care about the ones in this house, that I'm responsible for. You're already going through your own struggles; you can't be there to save everyone else if you're already struggling to save yourself, you trying to save everyone is going to result in you over-extending your own mind, and you'll end up suffering for it. On top of that, look at Zeb, he has no idea that he should be upset and not okay with you having your ex-boyfriend in your phone, when you weren't allowed to have him in it. That's not okay Tanna, that's not okay at all."

"Parker is right Tanna, though he said that a little crudely. He wants you to focus on getting your own mental state right, instead of feeling the pressure of having to be there for other people," Clemmy said reasonably.

I glanced at Zeb; he was still just sitting there smiling. I don't think he minded at all. What he just learned didn't bother him in any way. I knew what I had to do to appease Parker and Zeb if any seeds of doubt were growing in his mind.

"You're right, I will remove him from my phone right now."

"Oh Tanna, I'm not telling you to remove him from your phone, and I'm not telling you that you can't be friends with this guy, I'm just trying to get you to see that, when you're in a relationship, you have to be able to take into consideration your partner."

"No, I'm going to remove him, and I want Zeb to see." I held the phone out towards Zeb as I swiped the delete contact option on my phone. I knew it was just a gesture, I wasn't actually deleting anything but a shell. The messages were still in my messenger app, so I could always re-add him later. I'll just add him as a different name. This seemed to appease Parker, though he still eyed me suspiciously. I was going to have to watch my steps very closely if I was going to pull the wool over the eyes of Clemmy and Parker.

Chapter 10
Zeb

Zeb and I spent a few days getting to know each other the more traditional way. We sat down and talked about everything we could think of. It was Thursday, and we were discussing some of the finer aspects of bowling. He was still trying to convince me to give bowling another try, because it was his favorite past time. I just couldn't bring myself to find bowling appealing. I would rather sit and "watch" him bowl while I fiddled around on my phone. I could do things on my phone like rebuilding my group messaging forums. I only managed to recontact Lucky, none of my other contacts in the group messaging app returned my messages. This was all well and good, because I started regrowing my group, screening the people I allowed in. I had a target age and sex group that I found to be the most pliable, so anyone who didn't fall into those categories, weren't allowed in.

His head dropped a little and it appeared as if he was staring through the floor, instead of at it. "I like bowling so much because it reminds me of Alaska, it reminds me of my family, and my dad likes bowling."

I could tell that this was a moment, a fluctuation in the standard level of communication that Zeb and I normally held. It was deeper, softer. There was more hurt here. I hesitated, not knowing what to say, so I said nothing. He would take this step of his own volition; I would not force him into it.

"You know, when my mom and dad got divorced, I was five. I didn't understand why we had to go away, and my dad wouldn't come with us. My mom took Emma and me to Nebraska, and my dad stayed here, in Arkansas. It was years before my dad explained to me what actually happened. Years that I blamed myself for them splitting up. I always thought that me, a five-year old little boy, was to blame for my parents' divorce. If only I had been better, acted better, or been well behaved. My dad found out that I blamed myself, and he wept. He explained it to me, that it wasn't my fault, it's never been my fault. That sometimes people don't get along, sometimes they are better off apart." He took a deep breath, eyes brimmed with unshed tears. "I didn't fully understand it at the time, though I do now. Healthy relationships aren't always sunshine and rainbows, sometimes people fight and argue, but it's how they get through that mess, that determines whether it's a good relationship or not."

I nodded and rested my hand on his leg. I knew he didn't like skin on skin contact, but he wore some gray joggers. Having clothing between the skin and skin contact made his aversion practically non-existent. I wanted him to know that I was here if he needed me, that I wasn't going anywhere. I realized that this moment may be the first time I've ever been there for someone else, without an underlying ulterior motive. I mean, there was an ulterior motive, but it had nothing to do with this very moment.

"I was bullied, from the time I turned six, until the

day I left Omaha, and moved here with my dad. Every day at school, I would be picked on by the other kids, and then I'd go home, and later on be picked on by my sister's friends. It didn't help that I got held back in kindergarten because they said I was not emotionally ready to move on to the first grade. My mom did the best she could, but she had to work a lot, so she wasn't around to…to save me. I love my mom and my sister; I just needed my dad. My last school year in Omaha had me contemplating taking my own life. I just couldn't do it anymore. I was full of those thoughts when I came out to Arkansas to spend the summer with my dad. I was fourteen. He noticed that I was a little extra sensitive to everything. Then, two nights before I had to go back to Nebraska, I lost it. I was really down in the dumps, bawling my eyes out. I didn't want to go back; I couldn't go back. If I went back, I wasn't going to survive it. My dad had asked me what was wrong, and I told him. I told him that I couldn't live there anymore, that I was always hungry and bullied, that I was always sad, and always thinking about taking my own life. I didn't want to do that, I wanted to live, I just didn't know how I could live with being bullied every single day, I didn't know how I could live with being bullied and being hungry."

Zeb took another deep breath. "My dad had no idea that I was hungry, that the only time I got to eat, my small place of peace, was my small job at the bowling alley. I worked there, fixing the lanes and helping out with cleaning the tables. I got paid minimum wage for working there, but I also got to eat. I worked every single day they allowed.

"My dad was terribly upset about finding some of

this stuff out, and he blamed himself for not being more involved, for not being around more. He was paying my mom a fairly significant amount in child support, but living and raising two children alone, as a single mom, is an exceedingly difficult job. No one blamed my mom, not really. She did her best. He gave her a phone call and broached the topic of me moving in with him, here in Arkansas. He assured her he would continue to pay child support for me, that it wasn't about the money, but my mental health. She couldn't argue or disagree. Afterall, this was the best place for me.

"Since moving here, I've filled out my bones a little bit, and am a thousand percent happier. Sometimes, it's just the right environment that makes all the difference. I am no longer bullied, I get to eat every day, and I got a great job. To top all of it off, I met you. You really are amazing Tanna."

I smiled, looking at his sparkling green eyes. They were no longer showing signs of sadness, but of hope. He had hope for us. I felt my heart twist, a knot in my stomach forming as I fell a little further in love with him.

"Zeb...I...love you."

"I love you too Tanna. I have since I met you, I think. I recognized that where you're broken, I'm whole, and where I'm broken, you're whole. Together we make a whole piece." He kissed me, pulling me close. I felt real love for the first time in my life. It was surreal.

"I have a confession to make Tanna. You are the first girlfriend I've ever had, the first girl I've ever kissed, and the first girl I've ever loved," Zeb said with a blush.

"Oh, I could tell," I giggled, "and it's okay. You're only the second boy I've ever kissed, and I've never loved anyone else before. So, we are both experiencing the same thing for the first time."

Poor Zeb, he had no idea that I was very experienced. I've kissed a great many boys and have done far more besides. I knew that there was no way he would ever find out though, and that in itself, was worth my weight in gold. I could tell that Zeb was a true great catch. He was great looking, reclusive, incredibly hard working, and dedicated. In spite of all that, I felt like I could still do better than him, after all, I really was amazing.

Chapter 11
Alone

Everyone had Friday off from work and school. It was the Friday before thanksgiving break, and the teachers called for a conference. That morning, Parker and Clemmy were standing in the kitchen preparing breakfast when I walked in. Parker was standing shirtless in some red plaid pajama pants, and Clemmy in a big fluffy black robe. I sat down in one of the tall chairs at the bar.

"Good morning sweetheart, how did you sleep?" Clemmy greeted me with a smile.

"G'morning, I slept good. What are you making for breakfast?"

"Pancakes. How many do you want?"

Parker used a turner and flipped over a hotcake in a frying pan. I noticed some black specks in the dough, and asked curiously what they were.

"What's in that?"

"Chocolate Chips."

"That sounds delicious, I'll take two for now, and some bacon please."

"Not a problem, girly."

Parker handed me a couple of flapjacks and a couple strips of bacon. Pouring copious amounts of syrup on them, I began to eat. Parker turned the stove off, and left the kitchen, singing some random song that happened to dance across his mind.

"Okay Tanna, Parker and I discussed this, and we wanted to touch on a few subjects with you. You know that he and I are going to be going on a date tonight, we will be spending the night out in Hot Springs. He's going to have a little talk with Zeb, but I wanted to touch bases with you, about a couple of things. You've been here for a little over a week now, and I haven't asked if you needed any pads or tampons. I keep them in the medicine cabinet in the hallway, that's the tall skinny cabinet about halfway down the hall on the right."

I interrupted quickly, "Oh I don't need pads or tampons, my birth control makes it to where I don't have my periods." I thought about it for a second, well, it did, but I haven't taken my birth control since I left my mom and dad's house. I was not putting any more chemicals in my body. I wasn't going to tell Clemmy though, she has a master's in dietetics and nutrition, and would be pretty emphatic with me taking my medications.

"Okay good, well if you do happen to need any anyway, I keep a variety of them in the hallway. Zeb's little sister Emma is coming into town on Sunday, so you'll get to meet her. She's super sweet and nice, you'll love her to death. Last thing I wanted to talk to you about was using protection if you and Zeb decide to have sex. Always, always, always, use protection. You do not want to be a teenage mother, trying to figure out life. You have enough on your plate as it is. Parker and I do not want to be grandparents this soon either. We are not so naïve to think that you two hormone driven teenagers aren't going to be experimenting or figuring things out, so we want to make sure you two are adequately aware to use protection. I went ahead and ordered some condoms; they'll be delivered today. It's not us encouraging you to have sex, it's us making sure that if you do decide to, you are both properly prepared to be the safest possible. So please, use protection."

I stared at her, at first in shock, and then I burst into laughter.

"That's just gross. We aren't ready for that! We just started seeing each other. You don't have anything to worry about," I said quickly and almost too eagerly. Unbeknownst to me, Zeb was getting a very similar talk from his father in the other room. Except his dad was a bit more colorful when telling him.

"Condoms will be here today, when y'all decide to have sex, don't be a dumbass and go without wrapping it. Wrap it up. I don't want to be a grandfather for at least 7 more years, you got me?"

"Yeah dad, we aren't going to be doing anything like that, don't worry."

"Mhmm, just wrap it up."

That afternoon, everyone said our goodbyes to Parker and Clemmy as they went on their little mini-getaway date. I think they said something about making last minute reservations at a cabin down in the woods near Hot Springs. It was a strange feeling, but one of accomplishment and victory. Being left at the house with Zeb and his little brother Des showed a lot of trust. It's not a complete victory, because they already trust Zeb completely, but still, as a small victory, I'll take it.

The three of us that were left at the house were doing our own thing for now. Zeb was playing a game on his computer, talking with one of his friends, Des was in his room talking to his cousin and playing on his phone, and I was lounging around on Zeb's bed, messaging people.

-Me: Hey JP, what are you doing?

-JP: Hey Tanna, nothing, just hanging out at the house playing the new NBA basketball game.

-Me: Ah okay, I'm just laying in bed, not doing anything. Bored really, I want to make moves on Zeb, but you know, he's busy.

-JP: Just go sit in his lap, it'll get him going, it works 100% of the time, I promise.

-Me: Nah, I don't want to push him right now. It's our first night without any parents in the house, so I got plenty of time. We will see how it goes.

-JP: Oooo you're going to have a fun night.

-Me: Stooop. I wish it was you instead.

-JP: Yeah, but we both know how that turned out the last time, my parents won't even let me date anyone, let alone have anyone over.

-Me: I get it, but still. I got to go; I'll talk to you later.

-JP: Cya.

I stretched then got up and walked towards Zeb. I ran my finger along the back of his chair and kissed the top of his head. He looked up at me and smiled. I smiled back, and then walked out of his room. I figured I would go grab me one of the sweet snacks that Clemmy had in her Hot Cocoa bar. I grabbed a small white Christmas tree cupcake, a gingerbread man, and a Nutterbutter bar. I sure did like my sweets.

Des came into the kitchen to grab another slice of pizza or two. He looked at me, made a goofy face, and asked me what I was doing. His face twitched another time or two, but it didn't look silly. Des had Tourette Syndrome, he didn't do the verbal compulsions, but body and facial movements. Sometimes he would make random noises, but for the most part, it was just facial tics. He was very sensitive about it, and understandably so.

"What are you doing Tanna?"

"Grabbing a snack goob, what are you doing?"

"Grabbing a slice of pizza super-goob, I thought that was obvious with me eating it."

I squinted my eyes at him playfully and stuck my pinky finger out at him. It was a cute way I was flipping him off, without actually flipping him off. He set his slice of pizza back on his plate after taking a bite, then whipped both of his pinky fingers at me. He then quickly picked up his plate and strode back off into his bedroom. I thought about telling him that he wasn't supposed to eat in his room, that his mom would be livid if she caught him, but I didn't. Who was I to tell him not to eat in his room? I laughed out loud, that would be funny if I told him he wasn't allowed to eat in his bedroom, then went to Zeb's room and ate all my snacks.

I shoved my snack wrappers down the crack between the headboard and the bed. Clemmy was wondering about where all the snacks went and tended to blame Des and Zeb for eating them all. Since I was the only other girl in the house, she overlooked some of the things that I did. I had taken the bulk of my wrappers, and shoved them in the cabinet in the den, where I slept. There were so many wrappers in there, I was worried that the door wouldn't be able to properly shut. I knew that my ruse could not last forever, eventually Clemmy would get in there to grab one of her Christmas figurines, or Parker would go in there to get one of his whiskey bottles and glasses. I'd have to get that trash out of there at some point.

Zeb and I were watching a movie when he checked his watch. It was nine, he knew he had to get up and tell his little brother it was time for bed. He hopped out of bed and went and told Des that it was bedtime, and then he wandered around the house, shutting off all the lights and making sure all the doors were locked. It was pretty responsible of him to do all of that, almost like he was a grumpy middle-aged dad, complaining that he wasn't paying to heat or cool the outside, or complaining that electricity isn't free. It gave me a wry smile to consider that.

Walking through the door Zeb said, "Okay, he's in bed, he usually falls asleep pretty quick. His medication usually makes him pretty tired."

I patted the bed again. "Come here, let's finish watching our movie."

"Alright."

Zeb laid down next to me, and we finished watching one of those alternate dimensional shows on *Netflix*. With the credits scrolling by, I leaned into Zeb a little more and looked at him, he turned his head and gazed deeply into my eyes. We didn't speak, we both knew where this was going. He leaned in and kissed me, long and passionately.

It was different this time, I felt like it was more tender, and love filled than a bunch of random pinching and pulling. A far cry different than every other time I've experienced this in the past. Even with the Virginia man, it was almost rushed, like he knew what he was doing was incredibly illegal, so he had to get his and then hurry on out the door before he got caught. I wonder if he's still out there, taking advantage of little girls. I smirked, knowing that he was doing exactly that. He would be caught and punished for it, eventually. Then, likely, in some prison somewhere, the inmates would castrate him for his filthy mind, severing his capability to ever commit such a crime again. It's possible they would even murder him, shanking him over and over again, for the despicable nature of his crimes. I cared little what actually happened to him, let him die.

It wasn't a nice feeling, being left alone and at my own devices. Zeb had gone to sleep, Des was asleep, and I was awake, my mind stirring and creeping. I did think that I really loved Zeb, and deep down, I don't think I actually deserved him, not the other way around. I was damaged goods, I was a ruined corpse, my heart and blood just didn't know that I was dead. My family left me alone, my foster parents left me alone, my adopted parents left me alone. Every person in my entire life has left me, all alone. It's really what I deserved. I wept, silently. I was lying down in the den now, my own tiny little private secluded island. I cried for all the times that I was lost, for all the times that I was left. My tears were the last thing that left me alone, drying in the cool air of the house, leaving behind the gentle smell and taste of salt. I wondered then, just how long it would be, until Zeb and his entire family left me all alone. I knew it was just a matter of time. I hardened my heart then, my mind a vice of steel and resolve. It didn't matter what I did, I was going to be abandoned, so why not get what I wanted, do what I wanted, and be whoever I wanted.

Chapter 12
Unannounced

Des woke me up Saturday morning to the sounds him getting himself some cereal for breakfast. I groaned and rolled over. I was up until the wee hours of the morning, wallowing in my own self-pity. My groan was an attempt to let Des know that I was still sleeping, and that I could hear him being noisy. By the time he recognized that he had woke me up, he whispered "sorry" and then went back to eating his breakfast. I guess having someone sleeping in the den was still new to more people than I had considered.

I rolled to my feet, off of the little bed, and waddled into the kitchen. I nudged Des as I walked by him, he was still a little young for my flirtatious actions, but in a couple years, I could push that button a little. I had my boundaries, after all I wasn't a monster.

"Good morning, Des."

"Good morning, Tanna. You going to get some cereal?"

"Nah, not right now. I'm going to use the restroom and see if Zeb is up."

"He won't be up for hours! He normally sleeps until around noon."

"I'll just have to wake him up then," I said with a grin.

A few hours later, Parker and Clemmy came home from their little mini getaway. Parker came in and flopped heavily on the couch, grabbing the remote, and clicking on the television. It didn't take long for him to find the local football game; I assume he was listening to it in the car on their way home.

Clemmy went to the bedroom after saying hello to everyone. Five short minutes later, she returned and sat down close to her husband, and leaned into him. He gently put an arm around her and pulled her close. No words were exchanged, they just enjoyed each other's presence.

"How was your getaway mom? Did you guys bring me a souvenir?"

"No Des, we did not. We did have a wonderful time though."

"Can I go to the next getaway?"

"Well, the next one will probably be our family vacation trip to Florida, after school is released for the summer." Turning to me Clemmy continued, "By the way, in June we have a family vacation we try to do every year, to go to the beach in Florida for a week. You are officially invited, obviously. We will be taking two cars, one will have all of us girls in it, and the other will have all of the stinky boys in it. The girls coming will be you, Emma, her girlfriend Payton, my best friend Laura, and of course me. The boys will be Parker, Zeb, Des, Parker's best friend Bill, and Des's best friend Sam. We will be staying at a spot near the beach in Panama City."

I was shocked to be actually invited to their family vacation, which meant a lot to me. "Thank you! That sounds like so much fun! I'll have to start working on my tan in March."

"It's going to be a lot of fun. Also, as you know, Parker and Zeb are going to pick Emma up tomorrow. You don't have to go if you don't want to, but Zeb is going so he can see his mom. Do you want to stay home or go with them?"

"I'll go with them; I'd like to meet his mom too."

"Sounds good to me. Des will go too, so I can get a day of quiet all to myself." She stared off wistfully. "It's going to be wonderful."

The next day, at around five in the morning, Parker came through the house waking everyone up, so we could get on the road. It was a five-to-six-hour drive, and we had to be there by half past ten. We all piled into Parker's SUV and pulled out of the driveway. It was going to be a long drive, but we all had our phones and some pillows and a blanket so we could nap.

Around eight in the morning we pulled into a fast-food joint and grabbed some food for a quick breakfast. Occasionally, I would look down at my phone and see if I had any new notifications, but I knew that no one I actually wanted to talk to was going to be up this early on a Saturday.

Parker's phone got a notification over the car's speakers. It was their *RING* camera noticing some movement at the front door. Since we were all sitting in the car, not moving at this point, he grabbed his phone and checked the notification. I was sitting right behind him so I could see his phone clearly. There was a black SUV that had pulled into the driveway, and a small graying woman stepped out of the driver seat, and marched to the front door.

"Who the heck is that? Is that your mom Tanna?"

"That would be my mother, yes."

"I wonder why she's at the house, she must have been tracking your phone, and noticed you weren't home."

"Yeah, but I turned off the location stuff, but she probably got the address from before I turned it off."

"It's also possible that Clemmy invited her over, so they could discuss you."

I didn't know what to say to that, my mom could potentially be a kink in my chain, but I think it's more likely she will just say a bunch of stuff that falls on deaf ears. I wasn't too worried about it, as Parker and Clemmy have proven to be quite gullible when I tell them about my own significant woes. Parker put the vehicle in drive and pulled out on the highway, we had a long way to go still. I am a little curious as to why my mom would show up at the house unannounced.

Clemmy answered the ringing doorbell, surprised to see a woman she didn't recognize standing on the front porch. Judging by the nice clothes and the Cadillac SUV that was parked in the driveway, Clemmy had assumed it was someone here about Tanna, probably her mother.

"Hi, how can I help you?"

"I am Tori, Tanna's mom. Can I come in so we can talk?"

"Sure, come on in, my name is Clemmy, please excuse my comfortable appearance and my untidy home, I was not expecting company today."

The home was in fact quite tidy, and while Clemmy had the look of someone who was just lounging around, she was not inappropriately dressed. She had on a pair of red and black plaid pajama bottoms and a

Christmas hoodie top. She also sported some bright pink *Care Bear* house slippers that didn't match but looked incredibly warm.

"I'm here to discuss Tanna, and some of the issues we've had with her in the past, so that you all can be prepared to deal with that. There's a lot here to handle, and this may take a little while." Tori glanced at the large white sectional, almost as if she was requesting to sit.

"Please, let's sit down, do you want something to drink?"

"Some coffee would be great, no sugar is needed, just milk, thank you."

"Of course, give me a quick moment, I'll make you a cup."

Clemmy went into the kitchen and grabbed a coffee mug, placing it into the *Keurig*. It didn't take long, so Clemmy made them both a cup of coffee, and carried them back to the living room. Looking at Tori, she was dressed in a comfortable looking pantsuit, with black flats. It was very similar to something that Clemmy would wear to work. Tori was obviously there to discuss business, and she was definitely dressed the part.

"So, how do we start this off? Tanna has been sleeping in the den, Parker, my husband, put up a divider between the dining room and the den, so that she would have some privacy. She has access to her own bathroom, and her own bed and television. It's about the best we can do until we get the garage remodeled into an additional two bedrooms."

Tori nodded as if that was to be expected. "I sure do appreciate you letting her land here."

"Oh yeah, no problem."

"Most people wouldn't let some strange kid into their house for one night, let alone as long as she's been here."

"Well, I just wanted to make sure that she was safe, and had somewhere safe to be, since she couldn't be at home. My main objective with allowing her to stay here is that hopefully you guys will reconcile, and she can go home."

"She cannot come home; we do not want her to be in our house anymore. She creates nothing but discourse and drama and trouble in our home and it creates a lot of problems for my husband and me. It has been this way ever since she was about ten years old, so we've been dealing with this for about seven years now."

Clemmy considered Tori's tone and observed that Tori was very irritable and angry. It was obvious that she was at the end of her rope. It was very clear that Tori had had enough of Tanna.

"Just for some full disclosure, I work for the state, and I am a mandatory reporter. I had no choice in reporting the lock-out the next morning at work. I could lose my job and my entire career if I did not report it, and I cannot allow something like that to happen, over my sons' girlfriend."

Tori scoffed and said, "Yeah! I wouldn't lose my career over her either, she can go live in a box for all I care."

Speaking slowly and carefully choosing her words Clemmy said, "I think it's important that Tanna be in her home with her family. I think it's important for us to create an atmosphere of forgiveness so that she feels safe in coming back home."

Tori visibly bristled at the idea of what Clemmy was offering, becoming indignant she said, "She can come back, but if she did, there are rules in *my* home, and she would have to obey them. It's not like she would be allowed back home and be able to rule the roost again. She would have to earn all of her privileges, starting from scratch."

"So let me get this straight, if Tanna came home, would you allow her to continue to date Zeb?"

"No, she would not have her phone anymore, and he would not be in her phone when she got it back."

"So, you're telling me she would be coming back to that?"

"Yes."

Slowly Clemmy responded, "If Tanna knew that if she came back home that she would be grounded for the rest of her life, not allowed to see or speak to her boyfriend, there's no way she is going to choose to come back home, she's going to dig her little heels in and resist."

"You have no idea what we have been through with this girl. She talks to older men in chat rooms, I can't even let her have access to a school computer. She is prohibited by the school from having access to any of the school computers because of her past behaviors. I *had* to take away her phone because we couldn't trust her. She would sneak out to go meet up with people, she would disappear, she would stay up late at night, playing on her phone, then she would get terrible grades because she wouldn't be feeling well the next day. Half the time she isn't feeling good is because she isn't eating right. You should check her bag, I bet if you checked her bag, you would find all sorts of junk food wrappers stuffed in there. I imagine you will eventually find little hidden caches of junk food wrappers around your home."

Clemmy stopped her and said, "Ma'am, I'm a registered dietitian, so I do recognize that Tanna has disordered eating patterns, but she's seventeen years old, and at this point in life, it's not appropriate to put her on a diet. Especially when she isn't having major health issues related to her diet, but I digress. Right now, I'm not worried about what she eats or when she eats it. While talking to people online that are older than she is, is inappropriate, it totally makes sense with what she's dealt with as far as trauma in her past..."

Tori interrupted, "The trauma that she went through when she was a little girl has been made into such a big deal by all these counselors and therapists, and it just wasn't that bad. I've seen all kinds of people that dealt with so much worse trauma and abuse, and they turned out just fine."

Clemmy smiled and said, "Those people are the exception, Tanna is the rule. Not everybody is going to respond to trauma in the same way as the next person. When we experience trauma as a young child, it affects us by literally changing the way our body transcribes our DNA. This is related to something called Adverse Childhood Experiences, or ACES. The more ACES you have, such as parents getting a divorce, parents getting incarcerated, violence or drug use in the home, physical abuse or sexual abuse, the more of these markers that someone has, the more likely that they are going to have to deal with mental and physical issues."

With Tori showing interest, Clemmy continued,

"There's some really good research that you should look into that was performed by the CDC and Kaiser Permanente back in 1995. This is not brand-new research, although it's taken a very long time for it to be incorporated into health care. A good place to start would be the Ted Talk by Nadine Burke Harris, if you just google Ted Talk and her name, look for the one where she's in the red dress. I think it would be really good for you to hear what she has to say."

After taking the information down on her phone, Tori said, "I really wish that you guys would have Tanna turn the location back on her phone. At least then, I can watch where she's going, and know if she's somewhere she shouldn't be."

Clemmy nodded as if she was in agreement and would follow through with that.

Tori continued, "I also think you should go through her phone. I really think you would be shocked at the things you would find."

"Tori, I get that you're concerned, but as a parent, I'm not worried about going through a kid's phone. I understand that she's going to be flirting with boys and things like that. While I understand that that kind of behavior isn't healthy, per say, it's not trauma inappropriate or age inappropriate. So, unless she is doing something illegal, I'm not going to be digging through her phone and violating her privacy."

Bristling, Tori got defensive and began to slightly raise her voice, "You have no idea what it is like to have strange men stalking your home. You don't know what it's like to not feel safe in your own home because your daughter is inviting grown men over in the middle of the night. It's terrifying living in fear every single day."

Clemmy studied Tori for any signs of dishonesty and found none. It was obvious that Tori really did feel this way about Tanna's behavior. It was clear that there was some truth to Tori's words.

"Tori, we have security cameras at all entrances and exits of this house, including all the common areas. I am not concerned about someone coming or going from this home, without us knowing about it. My husband is perfectly prepared to defend this family and home by any means necessary. I have no fear that our family will be put into any danger."

"That's good, I'm glad to hear that. I'm glad that you have these systems in place." She took a sip of her coffee, realizing that what she was saying would only get her so far. "Well thank you for your time and the coffee Clemmy, let me get your phone number and let me give you mine so we can stay in contact about Tanna. She has a lot of medical needs and doctor appointments."

Clemmy wanted to reiterate her main point before Tori left, "Tori, my most important concern here is that she's able to come back home. In order for us to accomplish that, we must foster an environment of forgiveness and reconciliation."

Tori nodded and said, "Before I go, I wanted to caution you about one more thing. Your husband and Zeb need to be careful about Tanna, because she is hyper-sexualized."

Clemmy chuckled a little, and said, "Oh you don't need to worry about Zeb at all, he isn't like that. He is not hormonally driven, and my husband is never at the house during any of the times that she would be coming or going. I work remotely three days a week. He is already aware of the potential hazards of an unknown female being in the house and the potential accusations. He knows well enough to make sure he stays in the common areas when there was any chance of there being any one-on-one interactions."

Tori nodded and before stepping out the door said, "Those are good precautions to have. I will keep in touch."

Chapter 13
Emma

Back in the car heading towards Nevada, Missouri to pick up Emma for the Thanksgiving holidays, I was snoozing on and off. I was a little nervous about having another girl around that was my age. I don't know why, but usually girls my own age were able to see through my guise. I was also nervous because Parker had shown me pictures of Emma and she was incredibly beautiful. Prettier girls than me always made me either hate them or avoid them. I don't think I would be able to do either of these things with Emma, she was Zeb's little sister, and he cared about her very much.

At close to 10:30, we made it to the meeting point. Everyone got out and stretched their legs and headed into the gas station to use the restroom and find a small snack. Emma and her mom were still around fifteen minutes away, so we had plenty of time to get the blood flowing to our extremities. Parker went to fill the car up while Zeb, Des, and myself went to a big grassy area to continue stretching our legs.

"There they are!" Des yelled excitedly.

Zeb grinned and started walking to where his mother and sister had just parked. They were driving a small red Pontiac grand-am. When Zeb's mom got out of the car, I noticed her brassy red hair, and that she was very tall. When Emma got out of the car, my breath caught as I noticed how beautiful she was. Emma stood a little over six feet tall, she had strawberry blonde hair, and beautiful piercing blue eyes. She had braces on her teeth, and a big smile on her face. She wore a hoop in her septum and a couple of star shaped dangle earrings in her ears, and a couple of studs besides. She was thin, a runner's body. I learned that she liked to run cross country and play soccer. I also learned that she was pretty good at it too. Immediately, I was jealous of her looks. I would absolutely rule the world if I looked like her.

"Dad!" Emma shouted and ran towards her dad with her arms stretched out wide. "I missed you!"

Hugging her tightly, he said, "I missed you too sweetheart, gosh dang you get taller every time I see you."

"I think I'm almost as tall as Zeb now, I may even get taller than him one day," she said smugly.

"Yeah, that's probably not going to happen Emma. Most females stop growing around fourteen or fifteen years old."

Parker, Zeb, Emma, Zeb's mom, and I stood around in a little circle. Des was in the car, fiddling with his cell phone. "Mom, this is my girlfriend, Tanna."

"Hi Tanna, I'm Zeb and Emma's mom, Holly, it's nice to meet you."

"Hi Holly, really nice to meet you too."

"This is Emma, Zeb's little sister."

"Hi Emma, Nice to meet you as well."

"Hey Tanna." Emma looked at me, her eyes seemed like they could see right through to my soul. I see that she got her look from her father, as he seemed like he could look right through to my soul as well. Goosebumps went up my spine, I felt like I was a mouse under the gaze of a hawk that had just eaten. I wasn't in immediate danger, but I knew that I was being watched.

Riding home, I wasn't getting as much attention from Zeb as I wanted. I pretended to be asleep, every time we stopped, so that he would have to jar me awake. After the second time of me pretending to be asleep, giving a little groan when I was jostled, I distinctly heard Parker say, "She's not sleeping, just leave her alone, she doesn't need to go to the bathroom."

I'm not sure how he knew I was faking it, probably because of the switch in my breathing patterns. This family paid way too much attention to detail. Emma chuckled as she got out of the car. I opened my eyes as I realized I was alone in the car and everyone else was walking to the rest-area bathrooms. I watched as Parker and Emma gave each other shoves, when he shoved a little harder and she stumbled across the grass laughing, she came running back with her fist raised in the air in a silly attempt at a punch. They laughed and goofed off, and my heart sank.

I was saddened at the fact that I didn't have a relationship with my father the way Emma had with hers. Even with him not living near her, she goofed off and played with him like he was there every day. I'm sure she had a little bit of resentment for him not being in her life every day, but the love was clear to be seen. This was another reason why I was jealous, which caused my sadness to turn into hatred and fury. How come she got all of that, and I got nothing? It wasn't fair, she got beauty, love, and family, and I got disappointment, hate, and loneliness.

When they got back, I did not continue to pretend to be asleep. Fortunately, I didn't have to use the restroom, it was something I privately prided myself on. I could hold my need to vacate the waste from my body, both solid and liquid, for far longer than most people.

"How far away from the house are we Parker?"

"Yeah dad! How far away are we?" Des parroted.

"About forty-five minutes, depending on traffic."

"Des, Emma is going to get your bed, and you're going to be sleeping on the fold out futon in your room."

"That's fine with me."

"Emma, I'll get some different arrangements for Christmas when you and Payton come out. I look forward to meeting her."

"She looks forward to meeting you too Dad."

"Who is Payton?" I asked.

"Payton is Emma's girlfriend; she will be joining Emma when she comes out to visit for Christmas."

I looked at Emma, and she looked back at me, almost daring me to say something about her relationship with another female. I was raised differently, but I found myself looking at girls from time to time myself, so I didn't have anything inappropriate to say to her about it. My mom would be super judgmental, with her being hyper-religious, but I tended to stray a little from the "Good book."

When we got to the house, Parker grabbed all of Emma's luggage and toted it into the house. Emma ran inside and jump hugged Clemmy, obviously super excited to see her too. I mumbled incoherently under my breath about the injustices of life.

That evening Zeb was sitting at his computer playing some online games with his friends from Nebraska. I kept pestering him for attention, trying everything I could think of to get him to show me any sort of attention. I was met with very little success. I had one last trick to pull, so I sat in the bed, and I pulled out my little girl's tears. I trained myself a long time ago to be able to cry at will. I could produce exceptionally large crocodile tears and be very convincing.

Turning in his chair and muting his mic he looked at me. "Are you okay Tanna?" he asked gently.

"No," I cried, not giving him any information.

"What can I do to help?"

"I…don't…. know," still weeping and sobbing, I buried my head in the pillows and blankets.

He got up, stood there for a moment looking at me, unsure what to do, and then left the room. After a few minutes, he came back into the room, followed by his dad.

"Hey girly, what's the matter?" Parker asked.

I drew up some of my old, practiced excuses as to why I was upset, "I'm just thinking about my family, and why I have to go through all this."

"I can understand why that would be upsetting, but listen here Tanna, Zeb doesn't know how to handle all this. This is all new to him, if you're upset about something, as hard as it is, you have got to give him a chance to be there for you. Just like every man before him, he is unable to read the mind of the woman he loves. I take it you two have already said you loved each other, right?"

I sniffled, "Yes," and Zeb nodded.

"Okay then, think about it this way, as much as you are upset about the things in your past, you have something good going for you. Zeb loves you and you love him. That doesn't fix the world, but it's a little light that can brighten the darkened landscape around you. Focus on that, and you'll make your way through it. Zeb, put your arms around her and hold her until she feels better, okay?"

He sat down and wrapped me in a tight embrace. I buried my face into his chest and grinned, this worked like a charm. I knew that I could tug on the heartstrings with my traumatic past. People couldn't help but get soft hearts for a child who has been injured by things that were out of their control.

Emma had heard what was going on when she was heading to the bathroom, which just so happened to be right next to Zeb's bedroom. She frowned, not buying the attention seeking behavior that Tanna was putting on display. She couldn't put her finger on it, but she got a bad vibe and feeling from Tanna. Emma filed that feeling away, not wanting to be a thorn in her big brother's first real relationship. It was going to be an interesting thanksgiving week.

Chapter 14
Thanksgiving break

I knew it was going to be uncomfortable at the house having another girl my age there. It was exactly as I had expected, Emma saw through my actions, and saw the root of my behavior. She saw that I was petulant and starving for attention, that I acted out when I didn't get my way. I just acted out in a way that most people wouldn't recognize. I weaponized my past, my history, and I did so with impeccable success.

On the Monday before thanksgiving, Zeb had gone to work. Parker, Clemmy, and Emma were hanging out in the living room talking about Emma's plans for after high school. Emma wanted to be a commercial airline pilot. The local university was opening up a new pilot training program, which would make her dreams of becoming a pilot a bit more feasible and possible to achieve.

"Yeah, so if you decided to go to UCA and enter the pilot program, you could stay here, with us!" Parker exclaimed.

"Yeah! I actually have been considering that a lot. I really do want to come live with you dad, I've always lived with mom, now I want to come live with you for a while. If I could get a pilot's license as well, that would be an extra plus! Payton is considering coming with me, but she may not. She's really close with her parents, which is awesome. If I did come live with you and she decided to stay, I would just have to make lots of trips to see her whenever I could."

"Yep, and she would always be welcome here, whenever she wanted."

Parker and Clemmy had the biggest smiles on their faces, it was exactly what they wanted. They did their utmost not to show any favoritism of their children, and this was no different. It was just a dream of theirs to have their entire family at home, completing the circle. I noticed that no one had even looked in my direction since I came into the room, I was a simple fly on the wall, and I did not like that.

"I'm going to go to beauty school and develop clothes for animals after I graduate," I blurted out, a little louder than necessary.

With his eyes sparkling in amusement, "That's really good Tanna, I'm glad you have some goals for after you graduate."

"What kind of clothes are you going to try to design for animals?" Emma questioned.

"Are these animals someone's pet or wild animals?" Parker joked.

"Obviously not wild animals Parker, you goofus. Could you imagine her trying to seize a wild raccoon, the thing hissing and nipping at her the entire time she was trying to take measurements, it would be ridiculous." Clemmy chastised with laughter.

I giggled, "Of course it would be pets, mainly like dogs and cats, or horses. I want to go to beauty school to learn how to do makeup and stuff too, while I work on my pet clothing designs."

"There's a pretty good beauty school here in

Conway, if that's something you're interested in, we can definitely work on getting you enrolled after you graduate. Where do you plan on going after you graduate? Are you going to stay around here or move away?"

"I am going to be moving towards Dallas or Austin. There's a much larger market for what I want to do. I have done a bit of research on the career path," I lied.

Emma was looking at me without any expression on her face. I squirmed inside a little under her scrutiny. This girl knew very well that I was lying, and I just didn't know what I could do about that. How could I beat her gaze? In truth, I had no desires to do anything after high school, I wouldn't even graduate if it was up to me. I would marry someone who had money, and then live the rest of my life doing anything and everything that I wanted. All of these things I would ensure came to pass, it's just a matter of time.

After a moment of silence Emma said, "I think that's a pretty neat career choice Tanna, do you do any artwork, or do you draw a lot? It's my understanding that you need to have a pretty good handle on drawing for your designs to be accurate and able to be brought to life."

"I draw often, I really like drawing little mushroom forests and stuff. I think they are super cute."

"I like to draw too! Maybe we can sit down and draw some pictures sometime. I think it would be a good time."

"Okay! Let's do that today, do you want to Emma?"

"Sure! I brought my sketch pad, and pencils. I'll go get them."

Clemmy stood up and stretched, saying, "You girls

do that, I'm going to get some laundry done, then lay down and take a nap."

"And I am going to get my fishing gear ready, Bill and I are going to meet at the lake later and do a little catfish fishing."

I grabbed my little sketch book and a pen then wandered into the kitchen and sat down next to an already drawing Emma. I looked at her work and was amazed, she really had an incredible talent. She was drawing a face, I couldn't tell whose face it was quite yet, but the detail and circle-work was excellent. I have never, in all my life, been able to draw this well. I watched in amazement as the face she was working on began to take shape into a recognizable person. The eyes, even without color, were perfectly shaped, with each stroke of her pencil a new hair was put on the paper for her eyebrows. She was drawing Clemmy, smiling and free. The shading by her nose and under her lips was flawless. I decided then, I was not going to be drawing today. I was going to watch Emma until she was done drawing, then put my things away.

"What do you think?" Emma held up the completed facial profile of Clemmy with pride.

"It's amazing, how did you learn to draw that well?" I said with genuine amazement.

"It took a lot of practice and time by myself in my room. I spent a lot of time putting pencil to paper, because it calmed my mind and made me feel at peace. I really enjoy drawing," Emma said quietly.

"Me too," I said. Really, I just doodled, I drew a lot of mushrooms because they were easy, and I did think they were cute. Plus, my Lucky liked it when I drew them, and he really complimented me a lot when I did.

"Oooh wow! Is that Clem?" Parker came into the dining room and examined Emma's picture. "It looks so much like her, wow Emma, I'm going to hang this up and see how long it takes for Clemmy to notice."

Feeling kind of down, I went into Zeb's room and started texting Lucky. I knew he would answer, and I wanted to talk to someone.

-Me: Lucky Charms, what are you doing?

-Lucky: Hey beautiful! I'm not doing anything. I want to touch your clit and lick your tits.

-Me: lol

-Lucky: How are things going?

-Me: Just bored. Nothing is going on here. Want to face time?

-Lucky: Sure!

I got on the phone and spoke with Lucky for a couple hours, and just before Zeb got home, I was walking from the kitchen back to Zeb's room when Parker walked by and saw that I was talking to Lucky on face time. He eyed the phone for a moment, then looked at me, and walked away. I could tell that he was suspicious, but he didn't know how to approach it, so he just left it alone. I realized I was going to have to come up with a reasonable lie that he would buy.

I decided I would have to get ahead of this, so I got off the phone with Lucky, and waddled back into the living room where Parker was sitting down, getting ready to watch a movie. Emma was in Parker and Clemmy's room watching a scary movie with Clemmy, so I was alone with Parker for a few moments.

"Hey what are you about to watch?"

"Not sure yet, you wanna watch anything in

106

particular?"

"Nah, I'm going to go into the room with Zeb when he gets home, in like twenty minutes."

"I see. Let me ask you something, who was that boy you were face timing?"

"That's Lucky Charms, he's a fifteen-year-old boy from my support group that I've been helping out when he goes through some tough times with his homelife."

"Ah okay."

Parker seemed like he bought it, which left me feeling a little relieved. These people were so gullible, I could literally tell them anything, and they would believe it. This is going to make life for me really easy in the long run.

When Zeb got home, he immediately hopped in the shower, and deposited his filthy clothes in the washing machine. He had spent the day working on wheelchairs, and some of them had to be blasted with a pressure washer because they were covered in human feces. As the lowest man on the totem pole, he was required to do the least desirable jobs.

After getting cleaned up, I met him in his room. "Do you want to cuddle tonight and watch some more of the series we've been watching on Netflix?"

"Sure. Do you want to go on a little date with me? We can get some dinner and go on a walk at the park."

"Of course, I do!"

Zeb and I got dressed and went to one of the local Italian restaurants. Italian was both of our favorite type of food. His being a spaghetti and meatball meal, and mine being a chicken-parmesan. We laughed and goofed off all through dinner, it was nice having the entirety of his attention. After dinner, we went to a little walking park, and enjoyed a small stroll, just walking through the park under the lights that brightened the path.

"So, Emma is something else, isn't she?"

He looked at me questioningly. "What do you mean?"

I could tell that the original direction of me trying to turn him against her wasn't going to be a good move, at least not right now, so I just complimented her instead. "She's very talented. Her artistry is not to be denied."

He chuckled a little. "Yeah, she can draw really well. She has a bunch of talents, like singing, running, and acting. Emma is very charismatic."

"I can tell, I couldn't imagine having all that talent."

"She has her shortcomings too, but I'm her brother, I'm going to notice those more than most people."

"Like what?"

"Meh, it's not important, I'd rather talk about you. I heard that you're planning on getting a cosmetology degree. Then you want to work on designing clothes for pets? That sounds pretty awesome."

"Yeah! I think it would be super cool doing that. I really like animals, and I think I have a really good fashion sense."

"I agree with you, you always look amazing. I don't think I've seen a single one of your outfits that I didn't really like."

"Aww that's really sweet, thank you. What do you plan on doing after you graduate, I know we've touched on this a little bit in the past, you mentioned not going to college, and considering joining the Air National Guard, but is that still your plan?"

"Yeah, I still think I'm going to join the Air National Guard, but I changed my mind on the college thing. I think I am going to get a business degree with a focus on the stock market. I really like learning and playing the stock market, I've been putting money into it from every paycheck I get. Right now, about fifteen percent of each paycheck is invested. I've read quite a bit about it, and as young as I am, it will really prepare me for my future."

"Our future," I said with a smile. I wanted him to know that I planned on us being together for the long haul, and if he could be the one that would make lots of money and be able to provide for me, I'd stay with him.

"Yes, our future." He grinned.

In spite of all we did after he got home from work, we weren't out that late after dinner. It was only around seven o'clock, when we pulled back into the driveway. Going inside, Zeb hopped on his computer and started playing games with his friends.

"Hey, aren't we going to cuddle and watch our series?"

"Yep, I figured we would do that around eight thirty, this will let me still spend a little time with my friend Austin from Omaha. He was my best friend growing up, my only friend really. I told him we would be able to pick up on this game today, where we left off the other day."

I did not appreciate this, he was putting his friend before me, and that was unacceptable. He was looking at his screen when I flipped him off behind his back. I was scowling and glaring at him, this was not okay. How dare he choose his friends over me? How dare he not give me attention when we were together? I flopped down on the bed and grabbed a book to pretend to read. I told him and his family I liked reading, though I never really read often. I could tell by all the books around the house, all the different fully stocked shelves of books, that this family was one that read often. Inside my book, I placed my phone and started to text my friend Ruthelle from across town. Ruthelle was my only black friend, and really, I was only her friend because she had a fourteen-year-old little brother named Jeffon who had a crush on me.

-Me: Hey Ruthelle, what are you doing?

-Ruthelle: Hey Tanna, I'm not doing anything, just hanging out with my mom. What about you girl?

-Me: Oh nothing, being neglected and ignored by my boyfriend.

-Ruthelle: Girl, that's just not okay. Why is he neglecting and ignoring you?

-Me: Bcuz he would rather be playing video games than fondling me.

-Ruthelle: OMG that's messed up.

I took a quick picture of Zeb while he was sitting at his desk playing a game with Austin, and edited the photo, writing in huge white letters: "BRUH."

I then sent the picture to Ruthelle.

-Me: **Photo Sent**

-Ruthelle: that's just crazy. He is cute though.

-Me: That's about all he is, what kind of man neglects his girl when she is literally laying in his bed?

-Ruthelle: I don't know, I'm sure I could take a guess at a type or 2 lol.

-Me: Maybe I just need to ignore him and see if he will come find me. Sometimes that works right?

-Ruthelle: Mhmm girl, give that a try.

-Me: ok, I'll try it, talk to you later.

-Ruthelle: Talk to you later.

I got up out of bed and went to the living room where Emma and her dad were goofing off on *Mario Kart*. I didn't want to interrupt their fun, so I went ahead and went to my room in the den. I lay down and decided I'd pretend to take a nap until Zeb came and got me in an hour. I accidentally fell asleep.

Unbeknownst to me, Zeb came into the den approximately fifteen minutes later, he felt bad for not cuddling me when I wanted to, so he cut his game time short with his best friend. He tried to wake me up with a gentle shake and a kiss on the forehead. I didn't wake up, so he covered me with a blanket then went back to his bedroom.

The next morning, I woke up and realized that I was still in the den. Zeb had never come and woke me up, I was furious. I was going to punish him today, initially by giving him the cold shoulder. I figured I'd see where it went from there, and progress further if need be.

I got to my feet and went into the living room where Parker, Clemmy, and Emma were already up and about watching the news and playing around on their phones.

"Morning Sunshine, there's breakfast on the stove. I made some bacon and eggs."

"Thanks Parker, good morning. I'll eat in a few."

I went to the bathroom, and then peeked my head into Zeb's room where he was sound asleep. I didn't know how late he stayed up playing games, I just know that he ignored me, and lied to me about getting off the games at eight-thirty. I almost went into the bedroom and woke him up, but I figured he would probably be upset if I did that, so I went and ate breakfast instead.

"Do you want to go to Ultra Beauty with me today? I need to pick up some new eyeliner and just browse."

"Sure Emma, I'd love that."

I did not expect Emma to invite me to go to the store and shop for makeup with her, it was a pleasant surprise, and it almost changed my entire attitude about the previous night. I went into Zeb's closet and grabbed a small black dress, my pink Kirby hat, and some tennis shoes. This outfit was cute, it was perfect to go out on the town in. While I was getting my clothes, Zeb's alarm had gone off. I guess he had to go to work today, another way he could neglect me. He rolled over, smiled at me, and said, "Good morning beautiful."

I glared at him, didn't say a word and left the bedroom for the bathroom so I could change. I took a little time putting on my makeup, making sure I was extra beautiful so I could flaunt my looks to Zeb and make him wish he had spent more time with me. Unfortunately, I had spent too long getting ready, that he had already gone to work by the time I got out of the bathroom. I thought I had heard him knock and say something, but I was giving him the cold shoulder, so I ignored him.

Emma and I had a good time going to a couple of beauty and makeup stores. When we got done, I had spent most of my dwindling funds on a couple of new eyeliner pens, and some foundation. I also found a pair of thigh high white lace socks that I thought would go really well with the knee-high hooker-boots that Clemmy sometimes let me borrow.

Zeb had gotten home that evening, walked in the house, said hello to everyone and went to his bedroom. I did not acknowledge him getting home. I decided I would make it worse by going into his bedroom and sitting on his bed until he asked me what was wrong. Unfortunately, he didn't say anything to me. He got up and went into the living room while I sat there and sniffled, beginning to cry. How could he ignore me like that?

Parker asked Zeb, "What's going on?"

"I don't know dad, she's been giving me the cold shoulder all day, and ignoring me. Now she's just sitting in the bedroom crying, and honestly, I don't know what to do."

"Hmm, I will find out what's going on."

Parker and Clemmy walked into the bedroom, Zeb had stayed in the living room. "Hey girly, what's up?"

"Just feeling a little ignored by Zeb."

"What do you mean?" Clemmy asked.

"Well, he was supposed to cuddle with me yesterday, and he didn't, he just ignored me and played his stupid video games."

Parker shared a glance with Clemmy and then left the room.

"Tanna, I want to reiterate something with you sweetheart, if you don't feel like you're getting enough of what you need from Zeb, you don't have to stay with him to live here. You two don't need to be in a relationship to be together, okay?"

"I want to be with him, I just want him to want to be with me too."

"Tanna, Zeb does want to be with you. Have you two discussed what your love languages were?"

At this time, Zeb and Parker walked back into the bedroom. Zeb stood there awkwardly, and Parker flopped down in the computer chair at Zeb's desk.

"What's up?"

"I just asked Tanna if her and Zeb had discussed each other's love languages yet."

"We haven't yet."

"Tanna, can you guess what Zeb's love language is?"

"Acts of service?"

"Yes, and we can assume by your insistence that you two snuggle and cuddle a lot, that yours is physical touch, right?"

"Yes."

"Okay, so here's the deal, Zeb's physical touch is likely very low on his language list. That being said, Zeb, you need to be more aware that Tanna's love language is physical touch. I'm not saying do something you're uncomfortable with, I'm saying be mindful that she needs to be heard too. Just like you do, does that make sense?"

"Yes, it does."

"Yes."

"Okay, Zeb, we already told Tanna that if you two did not feel like you should be dating right now, or be together, she won't have to move out. You will have to be okay with her living here and not being your girlfriend if that's decided. No one is forcing you two to be in a relationship. I want that to be very clear."

"It is. I want to be in a relationship with her dad."

I looked at Zeb and said, "I also want to be in a relationship with you."

"Okay good, so you two should work out a plan on

how to deal with this. We righted the train, you two need to pull it into the trainyard. We love you both, so figure it out. Let's ease up on the drama a little and let everyone find their happiness."

Chapter 15
Thanksgiving

Thanksgiving Day was a flurry of activity. The kids all tried to stay out of the way of Clemmy and Parker, who were hustling around cooking food and setting the table. Clemmy was a huge organizer of wonderful things, especially the holidays. She liked her decorations to be on point. Clemmy did most of the cooking and organizing, directing Parker around at certain times when she needed a particular thing done that, she was too busy to do.

The centerpiece on the table was more of a Christmas arrangement than Thanksgiving. It was some holly berries on their branches laid out in an X pattern, with a round woven branch platter placed centrally on top of them. Sitting on the platter was a baby reindeer, its cute little legs folded up under it with its head raised in a curious way. Surrounding the platter was a bunch of small snow-flecked trees and a couple of tall candelabras. She would have the candles lit for dinner.

Tonight, we were having a beautiful pineapple glazed ham, and a perfectly salt-brined turkey. The assortment of sides were all delicious, with deviled eggs, mashed potatoes, collard greens, homemade mac-and-cheese, and corn on the cob. The homemade rolls were my absolute favorite, light and fluffy, with a crispy buttery top. I liked to sop up my giblet gravy with my rolls.

When we all sat down at the table to eat, we went around the table giving thanks for the things we each had. I was grateful for a lot more than what I had stated, but I figured simple flattery was the way to go.

"I'm thankful for my beautiful family. I love having my children here," Parker said, a small look of sadness glancing across his face. He missed his youngest son Ro, who was with his mother in another state. I haven't discussed the situation with him, but he somehow lost rights and privileges to him when Ro was little.

"I'm thankful for this wonderful life, and the opportunity to be happy with the people I love," Clemmy said cheerfully, she had noticed Parker's slight change in demeanor, he usually got a little down during the holidays, but he hid it well.

"I'M THANKFUL FOR THIS GOOOOOOD FOOD!!!" Des practically screamed, joy, happiness, and hunger on his face. It brought a small laugh to everyone around the table.

"I'm thankful for this family too!"

"Me too!"

I sat there listening to the repeated gratefulness, and then it was my turn, blushing I said, "I'm thankful for Parker and Clemmy for taking me in when I was at my lowest. I'm thankful for Zeb for being amazing and wonderful."

"Let's eat!"

We all began eating and chatting amongst ourselves, devouring the wonderful food. Each and every one of us showed our appreciation and gratitude to the cook. Clemmy took it all in stride, saying you're welcome

117

each time. After we ate our fill, dessert was on the counter for us all to enjoy. Parker didn't enjoy the different pies, even though an apple pie was made especially for him. He was a diabetic, and his last blood test showed him having an A1C of 12.9. This made him very aware of his intake of sugar, not to mention his wife being a registered dietitian.

After dinner, everyone was lounging around a little, Zeb was sitting in the living room with his family. I wanted to get him alone and have him to myself. I don't know why he would ever need to give attention to anyone else. I kept hinting at him to go to the bedroom with me and hang out.

Nudging him I said in a low whisper, "I'm going to go to the bedroom and kick my feet up for a little bit."

"Okay, love you."

I got up and slowly walked to the bedroom, looking back over my shoulder. He was focused on his conversation with his dad and Emma. They were talking about some board game that involved a bunch of different armies fighting over territories. I rolled my eyes then went to the bedroom. Looking at my phone, I had a couple messages on group messenger. Opening them up I saw I had one from a fourteen-year-old boy named Zachary.

-Zachary: Thank you for the invite into this group. I could really use some help sometimes; I get scared about some of the things that go on inside my head. Especially when my mom and dad fight, or yell at me.

-Me: You're welcome, Zachary, I'm going to call you Zach because it's a little easier to text. Is that okay?

-Zachary: Yes, that's fine. So, what all does this

group do? Is it just talking and helping each other out when we are hurting inside?"

-Me: Yes exactly. I am here to help you in <u>any</u> way that you need. Do you want to see a picture of me?

-Zachary: I guess?

-Me: Here. ***Picture sent***

I sent him a picture of me standing in the bathroom making duck-lips in the small black dress that I wore to homecoming. I thought I was very hot in this dress. It really made my "girls" pop out. I would get this boy all sorts hot and bothered.

-Zachary: Cool…

-Me: Where are you from?

-Zachary: I live in Mayflower, which isn't far from Conway.

-Me: Awesome, I live in Conway.

-Zachary: Cool.

-Me: Do you want to meet up sometime?

-Zachary: What… Why would you want to meet up with a fourteen-year-old boy? What in the world would I be even able to offer you? That's just crazy.

-Me: IDK

I immediately closed the app and shut my eyes. I thought, 'He must not like girls then. Oh well. I guess I'll just have to try someone else.'

-Me: Hey Kyle, what are you doing?

I sat there waiting for Kyle to respond. I figured he would definitely respond because of how bad he had it for me. Why wouldn't he? I was the woman of his dreams. After five minutes of being left on read, I scoffed audibly and slammed my phone down on the pillow. I decided to text Zeb and see if he would come to the bedroom.

-Me: Zeb, can you come to the bedroom really quick? I'm feeling kind of down because my mom and dad didn't invite me to their thanksgiving dinner, but they invited my brothers and their wives. I feel kind of left out.

-Zeb: Sure babe, I'll be right there.

Less than a minute later, Zeb came through the door. He came straight to me as I scrunched my face up, about to put on the waterworks. He wrapped his arms around me and held me close for a few moments before saying softly, "Hey, I got an idea. Come into the living room with the rest of the family, we are gonna play some board games, and we would all love it if you joined us."

I sniffled, "I would really rather stay in here with you, and just cuddle. Do you think we can do that?"

"I'm sorry Tanna, but not at this moment. I don't get to spend a lot of time with all my family. I think if you came and joined us in the living room for board games and fun, you would really enjoy yourself."

"I don't want to!" I said firmly, putting my foot down.

He smiled sadly at me, stood up, kissed me on the forehead and left the bedroom. Parker asked Zeb when he got to the living room if everything was okay. Zeb just shrugged, then walked into the kitchen with Parker following.

"What's the matter son?"

"Dad, she's acting like I don't give her enough attention, I really feel like I'm giving her so much attention." Zeb had the look of borderline panic on his face, a young man who was facing a problem he had never faced before, and not knowing how to handle it.

"Son, you are giving her plenty of attention. She's just been through a lot in her life, and sometimes will require more."

"But dad, I… I feel like I'm losing myself trying to give her everything she wants. I barely hang out with my friends online anymore, and when I do, I feel like she's upset or mad. I've been spending money like crazy, and I just want to keep saving."

Parker laughed, "Well son, the money thing, I have no solution for. Being in a relationship isn't cheap, you're going to spend money. I will talk to Clemmy about sitting down with her and discussing the aspect of saving, so that she can be aware of how important it is for you to be able to save. As for you losing yourself." Parker got a serious look on his face. "If you feel like you're losing yourself, you have to dial back on what you're giving. Don't give too much of yourself that you forget who you are. Play your games with your friends, she is becoming increasingly co-dependent on you, and it's not healthy. She will have to learn to find ways to entertain herself, there are plenty of things she can do around here that are hobby oriented. It's going to be okay, you are a great young man, don't stress yourself too much over it okay?"

With a look of relief on his face, Zeb gave a weak smile. "Okay dad, thank you."

"Good, now that all that is settled, do you want to play *RISK*!?"

"No dad, I want to *win RISK*!" Zeb said with a laugh.

"Good luck with that, if any of you kids want to beat me, you're going to have to earn it!"

Emma was sitting at the table setting up *RISK* with Des. She chuckled and looked at her dad and big brother. "Neither one of you is going to win, I'm going to kick all of your butts."

The games commenced with Emma taking the sloppy win. It was a lopsided battle; her secret mission was to defeat all of yellow's armies. Yellow was her little brother's army. No one knew each other's secret missions, so Parker was pummeling away at Des's troops and then ran out of armies. Emma went next and capitalized on the low troop count that remained for team yellow, winning the game.

"I WIN! HA! I TOLD YOU I WOULD WIN!" Emma gloated furiously, throwing her arms into the air.

"UGHHHH!!! I knew it! I knew you had defeat yellow!"

"Man, why was everyone picking on me!" Des shouted.

"Zeb was collecting all of Asia, I think he had capture all of Asia."

"Nope, I had to conquer 23 territories, Asia was just easy. Every time I got close though, one of you would knock me out of five or six countries."

I watched them play almost the entire game from the living room couch. I would look at Zeb from time to time, daring him to look at me. Now that the game was over, maybe he would come and hang out with me. I was his girlfriend after all.

"What game do y'all want to play now? Want to play munchkins?"

A chorus of, "YES!"

Parker got up and came into the living room to grab the next game they were going to be playing. He looked at me and said, "Tanna, come play this game with us, I think you would enjoy it. It's a good time."

"No thanks, I'm not feeling good, so I'm just going to hang out in here with Clemmy."

Clemmy was snoozing on the couch, enjoying her turkey-coma. I eyeballed her for a moment, pulled a blanket up to my chin and kicked my legs up on the couch. It would be fine; I would just scroll Tik-Tok and watch funny videos until they were done. I schooled my face so no one would know how much I was seething.

Scrolling through the videos, I noticed I had a new message down in my inbox. It was sent through Tik-Tok messenger. I opened it up and saw that it was from a man named Skylar.

-Skylar: Hey there beautiful, what are you doing?

-Me: Nothin much, what about you?

-Skylar: Just looking at you, you really are gorgeous. Where are you from?

-Me: I'm from Conway, Arkansas, where are you from?

-Skylar: Originally from Michigan, but I'm stationed in Africa right now for the marines.

-Me: How old are you?

-Skylar: I'm 47, single and ready to mingle. How about you?

-Me: I'm 17. Is that a problem?

-Skylar: Not a problem with me. Want to exchange pictures?

-Me: Sure! ***Picture sent***

I sent the same picture I had sent to Zachary from the support group.

-Skylar: Wow you're even more attractive than I thought!

-Skylar: ***Picture sent***

-Me: That's… wow.

Skylar had sent me a picture of his man-member. It wasn't the first dick-pic I've gotten, but it was definitely the most surprising. I did not expect a random man I'd been talking to on Tik-Tok for five minutes, to be so brass. I was pleased I still had that effect on people.

-Skylar: You like that eh?

-Me: Yea, actually I do.

-Skylar: You want to send me one?

-Me: Maybe later. I don't have a lot of money; would you buy one?

-Skylar: I could probably give you a little money, you give me your tag, and I'll send you some cash.

-Me: It's TannaBanana#23322 on the cash app one.

-Skylar: You should have the money now.

I checked, and I was pleasantly surprised that I did indeed have a couple hundred dollars in my account now. This guy really sent me money just like that, he didn't even know me. I could ghost him and keep the money without ever coming through with my end of the bargain. Whatever, I'll send him a dirty pic, but nothing too dirty.

-Me: Give me a moment.

I got up and went to the bathroom. I took a picture of my cleavage as I leaned over the counter. It would have to do for now, I didn't want to have someone accidently catch me doing this, I would probably send him something dirtier tonight. Afterall, he did deliver with the money, and the picture.

-Me: ***Picture sent***

-Skylar: Yeah baby, that's really good, how about a

little more skin now?

-Me: That's all for now, maybe I'll send you another one later tonight, it's still kind of early.

-Skylar: Come on, just send one really quick.

-Me: No. Later.

I closed out the app and went back to the living room. That was a weird exchange, even for me. Usually, I am looking for a local guy, but this was one all the way across the world. It still stroked my ego, so I wasn't going to complain, my mood was immediately improved.

After the games the family was playing, everyone started winding down for bed. It was almost nine o'clock and everyone was very tired. I went to Zeb's room, gave him a hug and a kiss and went back to the den. I forgot about the marine named Skylar in Africa who I was supposed to send a dirty picture to, and quickly fell asleep. This Thanksgiving Day was officially in the books.

Chapter 16
A Day with Clemmy

It was dark, I heard sounds of people shuffling around in the living room and the kitchen. Getting out of bed, I quickly used the bathroom in the laundry room and stuck my head out of the wall divider. Parker was drinking some unsweetened tea while Emma gathered up her things. She was heading back to Nebraska today, because she had to work tomorrow.

"Bye Emma, it was really nice meeting you."

"Bye Tanna, be nice to Zeb. I'll see you around Christmas."

I wasn't sure how I felt about having Emma come back for Christmas and New Years, she was very intimidating. It also meant that I would have to share Zeb's attention with his family again, while they have their many different "game nights."

"Unless you want to come with us, Tanna?"

"No thanks Parker, I will just hang out with Clemmy today."

Fifteen minutes later, Parker, Zeb, Emma, and Des were gone. Clemmy wasn't going to be up for another hour, so I grabbed a quick bowl of cereal then lay back down to take a quick nap. I loved taking little naps, even if I wasn't that tired. I called it my beauty rest. My quick nap turned into four hours, and I relished every moment of it.

Clemmy stuck her head into the den and said, "Hey Tanna, you up hon?"

"Yes ma'am," I said politely.

"Good, do you want to go get some Starbucks with me, then come back and do our nails?"

"Yes, I so very much would like to do that."

"Good! We will have a girl's day!"

I got dressed fairly quickly in a pair of sweatpants and one of Zeb's hoodies. Clemmy met me out in the car, and we left right afterwards.

"So, what do you like to drink from Starbucks?"

"I like a mocha Frappuccino with vanilla bean powder."

"Oh, that sounds delicious, I get a caramel ribbon crunch Frappuccino. Sometimes I will even add an extra shot of espresso or two, when I'm feeling extra low on energy."

We got our drinks and made it back to the house. As we were putting on the nails, we had bought a couple weeks ago, Clemmy decided to talk to me about her past.

"I don't know if you know this, but I went through a lot of traumatic experiences as a child too. I know it looks like I got all my stuff together now, but my entire life has been a total mess. It started the day I was born, my mom has schizophrenia, and growing up she didn't even have the wherewithal to even care for my hair, let alone my entire being. My father had to work a lot in order to take care of both of us. She would neglect me while he was gone, he would put me in my crib with a bottle in the morning, and when he would return, the bottle would be nearly empty with soured formula sloshing around inside the bottle. I sometimes could be found lying in the crib in my own excrement, completely covered head to toe with it. It was so bad that I would often reach inside my diaper and smear it on the wall so that I could get it off of my skin. I would scream for so long trying to get my mother to come to me, that by the time my father got home from work, my voice would be raspy and hoarse. There are even photos of my mother holding me as an infant, and I had this totally blank flat affect on my face because I was so mal adjusted from being neglected so much. I remember my dad taking me to hair salons once a year, to get my hair brushed out, because he didn't know how to braid a girl's hair. My hair was so thick and curly, and my mom wasn't able to do anything with it because she was so out of it.

"We lived with roaches, rats, spiders, and all sorts of other vermin. The mold in the house was so thick, I would get lung and ear infections all the time. We had military insurance and they refused to remove my tonsils until I was sixteen years old. I remember being hungry all the time because we couldn't afford food. My dad would have to try to get what he could from the food bank. I remember we had to take the bus everywhere because we didn't have a car. We would have to take our dirty laundry to the laundry mat across town in these metal carts, while riding the bus.

"My mom used to abuse me because she was so far out of it with her mental disorder, I was never safe at home growing up. To say that my father was any better than my mother would be a lie. My father is a pedophile with a serious gambling problem. I was abandoned by my parents and left with my grandmother for years. I say all this to tell you that I can relate and understand some of what you have been through. I wanted to let you know that I used to be a lot like you, I see that you like to get the attention of boys, and I mean a lot Tanna. While it may make you feel good in the moment, I promise you, it will not make you feel fulfilled in the end. You need to know that all of these boys are just after your body. They are not after your mind, or to get to know who you are. They are after one thing, and one thing alone.

"Zeb on the other hand, he wants to get to know you. He wants real love, not lust. He is not hormonally driven, he is driven by companionship. I don't really know what to say to you as a Forty-two-year-old woman, but I need you to understand that you are enough, and you do not have to use your body to get the love and attention that you desire."

My eyes welled up with tears, as I finally felt like someone truly understood me for exactly who I was. She came over and hugged me, holding me tightly she said, "You are enough, you are brilliant, you are beautiful, and you don't need boys to make you feel good about yourself. You are already enough."

I didn't know what to say, I didn't know what to do, so I stood there and wept. I wept because I thought there was no fixing me, that I couldn't recover from what I had become, but here I was looking at a woman who was not broken anymore, who had recovered from her life. I finally felt like I wasn't alone in this world. I finally felt like I had hope.

We sat and talked about the little things after that. It was nice to be able to connect with someone on that level and find companionship. Clemmy was everything I could ever want in a parental figure. I wondered if I could get Clemmy to get guardianship of me. I'm sure my parents would allow that to happen, without any sort of fight at all. They just didn't want the responsibility of someone like me under their roof anymore.

At four in the afternoon, Parker pulled back into the driveway with Zeb and Des. They had made the trip safely and got Emma dropped back off with her mom. I rushed out the door and threw my arms out wide towards Zeb, hoping that he would take me into his embrace. Zeb wrapped me up in a quick hug and asked, "How was your day?"

"I had a really good day with Clemmy. We really connected a lot. She's pretty amazing. You have really awesome parents Zeb."

"Yeah I know, but don't say that too loudly, they'll let it go to their heads."

That evening, Zeb and I lay in his bed watching our show on Netflix. We snuggled and cuddled until around ten that night, and he said, "I think you should probably head to your own bed now, I'm getting really tired."

Before I could answer I felt a buzz on my hip as my phone vibrated. I looked down and saw a message from Lucky. I decided that I wasn't going to get anything else from Zeb that night, so I nodded. I kissed him lightly and hopped out of bed and headed towards the den. I put my earbuds in, and face timed Lucky after reading his message.

-Lucky: I'm horny, face time me slut.

Lucky and I were in the middle of a phone-sex session through face time when I heard Parker and

Clemmy having a stern discussion in the living room. I couldn't tell what it was about, so I ignored them. Lucky had my full attention while he touched himself, and I touched myself. We whispered our reactions to each other, until we fell asleep, with facetime still going.

While I was sleeping Parker and Clemmy had made up and were having a conversation about the girl that was currently living with them. "I swear I heard her having phone sex when we were arguing in the living room."

"She was not Parker. I just had a talk with her about her worth, she wouldn't do that. Plus, you can't hear anything, you're practically deaf. How in the heck could you have heard her doing something like that."

"I don't know, but I know what I heard. I bet it with that Lucky kid, I'm telling you, something isn't feeling right about that entire situation. I don't trust her."

"She does talk to that boy a lot."

"I'm going to say something to her the next time I see her talking to him."

"Alright. Let's get some sleep, I love you, Parker."

"I love you too Clem. I always do, I'm sorry I'm such an ass sometimes."

"It's okay, I'm hard to deal with at times too."

Chapter 17
School

Saturday was relatively uneventful, I hung out with Zeb in his room all day. He spent the day alternating between playing video games and chatting with me. We went out to eat and watched television, switching between funny movies and an alternate dimension series on *Netflix*.

On Sunday, I asked Clemmy if I could go over and see my friend Ruthelle. It had been some time since I'd hung out with her, and I missed her company. She saw things how I saw things, at least how I told her things were going. Clemmy said no problem and took me over to Ruthelle's house and dropped me off. She had to run errands in town anyway, so it wasn't out of the way. I couldn't wait until I got my car out of the shop, which hopefully, should be sometime this week.

As I'm walking up to the front door of Ruthelle's house, I felt my phone vibrate in the purse hanging at my side. I'd check it later; I wanted to get inside and hang out with my best friend. The first thing I wanted to do when I got in there was to strut my stuff around Jeffon, Ruthelle's little brother. I liked to make him blush, which was super cute, even though as a person of color he did not blush much, there was just a small change in his hue, but could tell.

Jeffon met me at the door, with a big smile on his

face, he said, "Oh baby, am I glad to see you. It's been a long time since I had a taste. Girl, come here."

"Don't be ridiculous Jeffon," I said loudly, then whispered. "You better not have told anyone about that, I swear to God, I'll never let you even look at me again."

"I didn't tell anyone, I promise," he whispered back.

A month or two before I met Zeb, when I was still dating Kyle, I came over here to Ruthelle's house. I was hanging out with them when Ruthelle and her mom had to run to the store. Jeffon was only thirteen then, so they left me here to babysit him. One thing led to another, and I let him experiment with me. It was a nice change, and he liked to tell me how perfect I was, so I figured I'd reward him.

"I am not here for you today, Jeffon, I want to hang out with your sister. Where's she at?"

"She's in her room."

I headed down the hall to the last room on the left. Inside was a medium sized room with dark purple paint on the walls, and a mixed smattering of colored LED lights on the ceiling, which made it look like we were in space while lying on the bed. The curtains were a light purple, blackout style, and her bed had many different planets printed on the sheets and pillowcases. Ruthelle loved space; she had big plans to become an astronaut after college. She was the most intelligent person I knew at my school. Her grades put her in the running for valedictorian. Ruthelle was a senior and already had a full scholarship to go to several Ivy League schools.

Ruthelle herself was beautiful. She had a gorgeous dark coffee skin tone, with the most perfectly straight and white teeth. What really drew the eye was her blue eyes. They were like looking at the ocean on some desert island in the Caribbean. She was not very tall, only around five foot six, but she carried herself as if she were seven feet tall. I don't know why she didn't intimidate me or make me hate her because of her looks, like all the other beautiful girls did, perhaps it was because I had known her since I was adopted at seven. She went to the same church my parents had forced me to attend, before we had to change churches because of my behavior in the bushes with those boys.

"Hey Girl! What are you doing? It's so good to see you, it's been forever!"

"Hey Ruthelle! Yes! I'm so glad to see you too, I had to get out of the house, I was so bored. I got tired of being neglected and ignored by my man."

"I get that, I wouldn't stand for that either. It blows my mind that he doesn't show you any attention at all. I'm assuming you're only staying with him because it's allowing you to stay in that house and retain your freedom?"

"Yes, that's exactly right."

About then, my phone vibrated again in my purse. It was sitting on her side table, and it made a loud BRRRRRT sound as it bounced off the wood and leather. I had sat down at her desk while we were talking. I stood up and walked over to where my purse was and grabbed my phone out of it.

"I bet this is Zeb checking on me, probably concerned that I'm cheating on him or something," I said, rolling my eyes.

Looking at my phone I noticed I had two messages from my mom.

-Mom: Hey Tanna, I just wanted to remind you that you have a doctor's appointment at 8 am on Tuesday.

-Mom: I would appreciate it if you acknowledged this, I'd also like you to get ahold of the doctor and change your contact information from my number to yours, so you can keep track of when your appointments are.

I scoffed, "Ugh, my mom is so annoying. She texts me like she's being nice, but I know her. She's being super asinine and rude."

"What did she say?"

"Oh, just that I have a doctor's appointment on Tuesday, and to make sure while I was there, I had them change the contact information to my number because she was sick and tired of dealing with my appointments for me. She said, 'You want to be grown, then you better take care of your own stuff. Stop having them contact me.'"

"Dang that's kind of messed up, my mom would never be like that to me. She would always be super helpful and loving."

"Yeah, your mom is the absolute best. Where's she at?"

"She's working, I'm watching Jeffon today, to make sure he doesn't do anything stupid."

"That's a tough job," I joked, and we both laughed. We spent time together and spoke about Zeb and how it was living at his house with his family.

"Girl, they invited me to their family vacation to Florida. We are going for a whole week in June!"

"Wow! That's a real family there, that's love. They invited you because they welcomed you into their family, not just welcomed, but as a part of their family.

Tanna that means so much."

"Yeah, Clemmy is really awesome. Parker is okay, I don't think he trusts me very much, he's very suspicious of me. I can see him eyeballing me when I'm talking to some of my guy friends on face time. I help a lot of people out in support groups, these people get suicidal and really mentally struggle sometimes. I try to be a soft blanket for them."

"Parker sounds like he's very controlling."

"I haven't noticed much of that, but I guess the jury is still out. I met Zeb's little sister too, she's just like her dad. She's super intimidating, and always seems like she's hyper focused on everything around her, though Des, Zeb's little brother, he's just a goofy little boy. I love him to death; we get along great."

"Zeb's little sister doesn't live with you guys, right?"

"Correct, she lives in Nebraska with her and Zeb's mom."

"At least you don't have to deal with her all the time."

"Yeah, except she's coming back for Christmas Break. I got a few weeks for that still though, so it'll all be good."

Ruthelle and I spoke about other random things for another two hours until Clemmy sent me a text message letting me know she was outside, and was ready to head home. I gave Ruthelle a hug and left her room. Ruthelle didn't follow me out, so I swung by Jeffon's room, knocked on his door. When he hollered, "It's open." I pushed it open, and pulled my shirt up and flashed him, when he turned to look at me. His mouth dropped open, I grinned really big, then left the room, without saying a word.

Clemmy and I went home, and I was smiling inside. It was nice to hang out with Ruthelle, and even nicer to tease her little brother like that. Ruthelle didn't know everything that was going on at Zeb's, and I skewed a little of the truth, but I felt like it was easy to talk to her. I felt like I had a supporter in my corner, that she had my back.

"I have a doctor's appointment on Tuesday," I told Parker and Clemmy, who were sitting in the kitchen.

"Okay, what time? I have to work, and so does Clemmy."

"I think it's at 8:30 am."

"Okay hon, you will just have to take my car. I'm going to be working from home that day."

"Sounds good, thank you."

The next day, everyone got up and ready for school. Zeb drove me to school on the back of his motorcycle, and I lived for it. Classes were going fairly well, until I got a call to go to the office during my third period. I got there and saw my mom, standing at the front office, holding a stack of papers.

"Tanna, I have brought you emancipation paperwork. You want to be grown, you wanted to move out, well we don't want the responsibility of your decisions when you aren't living with us, to haunt us. Get these papers signed, notarized, and then send them back to me. I will have our family lawyer do the rest."

My mom was not being quiet, everyone in the office and the surrounding halls could clearly hear what she was saying. They all knew that I was not living at home anymore, and that my mom was declaring me emancipated. I was thoroughly embarrassed. I snatched the paperwork out of her hand, turned on my heel and left without saying a word to her. Before I even got around the end of the hallway, I was crying. I heard my mom yell after me before I went out of sight, "GET YOUR BIRTH CONTROL FILLED!" I felt sick to my stomach, and I did not want to be there anymore.

After feeling sick for an hour, I decided to go to the nurse and see if I could be released to go home. They refused without parental permission, knowing full well that I would not be able to get that from my mom and dad. I texted Clemmy to see if she could do something about it.

-Me: Clemmy, I'm very nauseous, I've thrown up a couple of times and I don't feel good. Can you come get me from school?

-Clemmy: Let me see what I can do.

-Clemmy: So, I called the school, and they told me only a parent or guardian can check you out. I called your mom, and she said you were probably faking it, and that she was not going to come get you from school. I'm so very sorry sweetheart, I don't know of anything else I can do right now.

-Me: Okay, thank you for trying.

This was bullshit, my mom knew what she did was going to make me feel ill. She knew that I wasn't going to be able to stay at the school today after she pulled that stunt with the emancipation paperwork and the birth control prescription. I'll just have to tough it out and think of another solution. My mind kept straying back to the guardianship stuff that I had considered before. I will ask Clemmy if she will apply for guardianship of me tonight, and we will see where that goes. In fact, I'll just text her right now.

-Me: Clemmy, do you think you could apply for guardianship of me? I think my mom and dad would be okay with it, if asked. My mom brought emancipation paperwork to the school today, I don't think she has any desire to make amends with me to get me back home.

-Clemmy: I can definitely look into that. Let me check with your mom and see what's going on. Now that the emancipation paperwork is in play, I don't think it would be an issue to convince them to allow us to take guardianship of you.

-Me: Thank you.

-Clemmy: Hey, sorry, I know it's been a few hours, but here's what I figured out. So, I did some research, and I spoke with your parents. I also spoke with a contact I have at DHS. Your mom and dad are on board with us getting guardianship of you, which is great news, because they would have been our biggest obstacle in getting this accomplished. Your mom is going to send over the notarized portion of the guardianship paperwork to me, and we can take it later this week to get our portion done.

-Clemmy: After that, we just need to take it to the clerk at the courthouse to have it filed, and it will be official. You will be my ward. It's pretty exciting if you ask me.

-Me: That is such a huge relief, I will sign anywhere you want me to. Just tell me when and where.

-Clemmy: Ok, well now that the ball is rolling for that, I do have one other thing to tell you about. With Zeb off to work, I'm at work, and Parker is at work, you're going to have to walk home today from school. Just cut through Laurell Park behind Juan Pepe's, and then it's only about another quarter of a mile.

-Me: Yeppers, Zeb showed me how, because he knew I was going to have to walk home today with all of y'all working.

-Clemmy: I also wanted to ask about your job at the green chicken. What happened with that? I noticed you haven't asked to go to work once in the couple of weeks you've been here.

-Me: I got fired for asking someone to work for me. Remember when Zeb and I went on a date a while back? Well, I was supposed to work that night, so I requested someone to swap with me. The manager called me back and told me not to bother returning, because I swap shifts too many times.

-Clemmy: Oh dear, well, unfortunately that will happen. Going to work is a commitment that needs to be honored. Don't worry about it, if you want to find another job, you're more than able. You should probably wait until you get your car back though. That should be this week sometime, right?

-Me: Yep, supposed to be ready on Thursday.

-Clemmy: ok good, well you enjoy the rest of your day at school, I'll see you when I get home. Love you.

-Me: See you when you get home! Love you!

Chapter 18
Elisha

I got home from school around Three forty-five. I rounded the corner at one end of the street, and I saw Des rounding the corner at the other end of the street. He rode the bus to a school that was across town. It had dropped him off a few moments ago, and now we were facing each other. He looked up, a few hundred yards away from me and noticed me. Stopping in his tracks, I stopped in mine too. As if we were thinking the same exact thing, we both bolted to the house, running as fast as our little legs would take us. I had a slight advantage in distance because I had a little less of it to go. He had an advantage in weight and athletic capability, my backpack was very heavy. It was full of books, scrap paper, and junk food trash. He also had an advantage that he didn't know about, and that was the fact that he didn't vape, and I did. I had my vape pen tucked safely and secretly away in my backpack, under a mountain of empty cookie wrappers.

With all his advantages, it was still too much for him to overcome the advantage I had in a shorter distance. I beat him to the front door just as he entered the yard. I placed my fingertip on the electric fingerprint reader and the door unlocked. Parker had installed the fingerprint reader and automatic door lock because crime was starting to increase a little in the city and he worked a lot of hours.

Stepping inside, I quickly turned around and shut the door, turning the lock so that Des would have to unlock it himself. I could hear him messing with it, mumbling between deep breaths that I had cheated because I didn't have as far to run. I laughed and yelled through the door, "I beat you! Suck it!"

"Yeah, yeah, yeah whatever," he said as he came through the door.

Des immediately went to work on his daily chores. He knew that if he didn't get his chores done before hopping on his phone or the video games, he would get in trouble. I don't think he appreciated getting in trouble and losing the privilege to play video games as often as he did.

After dropping my backpack off next to the coatrack, I flopped heavily on the couch. Archibald, the fat cat, mewled and hopped up into my lap. Cats were such sweet creatures, especially these ones. They just loved being scratched right behind their ears and under their chins.

Buzzzz buzz buzz

-Zeb: Hey Tanna, were you able to make it home safely?

-Me: Yep, just got home. I raced Des and won; he was a little slow. Lol.

-Zeb: Good!

-Zeb: My cousin Elisha, who I was raised with being pretty much my best friend, is supposed to be coming by tonight. I've been telling him a lot about you, and he wants to meet you. He just moved back into town from Georgia. He had spent some time living with his grandfather.

-Me: Okay. I'll go change and get appropriately dressed. 😊

-Zeb: I think you will look stunning no matter what you wear.

-Me: I bet you do, even when I'm not wearing anything right?

-Zeb: Even then. Got to get back to work, I love you.

-Me: I love you too.

I immediately got up from the couch and went to Zeb's bedroom. I had been storing my clothes that needed to be hung up, in his big closet. There was plenty of room, considering most of his clothes were shorts and hoodies.

I grabbed a short red skirt and a white low cut V neck top. I would make sure Zeb's cousin was jealous of Zeb.

An hour later Zeb was sitting next to me on the couch. We were sitting close, but not so close that my bare skin would touch the bare skin of his arms. I did test whether he was lying or not about his aversion to skin-on-skin contact, and I found myself stunned that he wasn't. I would put one fingertip on his arm, and his arm would immediately break out in goose flesh. I figured this test was inconclusive, so I tested again on his back after he had gotten out of the shower and just wore a pair of shorts. I put my hand on his back and had a similar result. His entire body broke out in goose flesh, and he squirmed. He didn't demand I not do that; I think he assumed his squirm and attempt at pulling away from my hand was enough to let me know to not do that. He wasn't wrong.

Motion was detected at the front door and Zeb

hopped to his feet quickly. He smiled big and walked to the door to verify that his cousin had arrived. When Zeb opened the door, a man walked in with a little girl. The little girl turned out to be his little sister Mae. The man immediately caught my eye, he wasn't tall, only about five foot nine inches, but he was thin with auburn hair and brown eyes. He had thick dark brown eyebrows and straight teeth. I stood behind and to the right of Zeb as Elisha came in. Zeb quickly wrapped Elisha in a hug, and fist bumped Mae. Mae was a pretty little girl, around eleven years old. She had long dark brown hair and a mischievous smile. I liked her immediately.

Motioning to me grandly, Zeb said, "Hey Eli, this is my girlfriend, my love, Tanna."

"Hi Tanna, I've heard a lot about you." Elisha took my hand and shook it.

"I've heard a lot about you too." I smiled big, locking eyes with Elisha.

Parker came into the living room and quickly wrapped Elisha and Mae in a hug. He had a big grin on his face as he said, "Hey Elisha, hey Mae. How are my niece and nephew doing today?"

"I prefer to be called Eli, Uncle Parker," Eli had said with a grin.

"Why? I've always called you Elisha. Is it because of how it's spelled? It looks too much like Alisha?"

"That's exactly why, if I write my full name out, people call me Alisha, and I'm not a fan of that. So, I just write out Eli."

"Makes sense. I'll call you Eli, no problem. How are you Mae, you're just as pretty as ever."

"Hi Uncle Parker, I'm doing good. I'm mad at my

mom right now because she won't let me go to public school. I have to keep going to that stupid private school."

Parker and Mae walked off to chit chat about the various woes of being an eleven-year-old girl. Zeb, Eli, and I were still standing by the door. Eli and Zeb were talking about Eli's job, he worked as a Door-Dash delivery driver.

"It doesn't pay a lot, but it gives me a little money to get around town and goof off with."

"That's important, I'd try to get you on where I work, but I don't think I've been there long enough to be able to do that."

"It's all good, I'll find a better job somewhere, no problem."

Looking at me, Eli leaned in towards Zeb and said, "Lemme talk to you privately in the room really quick."

"Okay, Tanna I'm going to go into the room and talk to Eli for a moment, is it ok if you stayed out here?" Zeb then leaned in closer to me and said, "Don't worry, I'll tell you all about it later. He's probably just being nosey." Zeb grinned as he made sure he said it loud enough for Eli to hear him. Eli just chuckled and walked into the bedroom, with Zeb following.

I went to the bathroom to make sure my make-up was good and straighten up my hair. I also had to let lose a little back-door air, and since I wasn't farting in front of Zeb or his family yet, little bathroom sneak offs worked well for me.

Eli was very charismatic, with an easy-going smile and a lazy gait to his stride when he walked. I was infatuated with him. I knew it was wrong because I was with his cousin and best friend Zeb, but Eli was a bad boy. He smoked cigarettes and weed, he got his GED, and he didn't care about authority. He did what he wanted.

"Do you two want to go to the O'Shallys and hang out? I'm done working for the day and I promised Mae, I'd take her to the arcade and buy her a pizza."

"Sure, we don't have anything going on today. Just got to be back by 9, because it's a school night."

"Right, I don't mind going, I like O'Shallys, they got a really good food menu."

"Hey Mae, time to go. I'll drive us. Tanna can sit in the back with Mae and you can sit up front with me Zeb."

"Okay."

We went to the arcade and ordered a pizza. It wasn't the best pizza that I had ever had, but it wasn't terrible. I kept watching Eli, his goofy bad-boy nature. It didn't quite fit him, though he held it fairly well. He was outgoing and hormonally driven in every way that Zeb was not. Zeb was reserved and focused on the future, he wanted to be organized and save money. Eli was about living in the moment right now. A tiny part of my brain was telling me to ignore him because the future was a lot longer than the moment.

As the night wore on and we lost a bucket load of quarters at the arcade, I grew a little bored of the bad-boy act. I quickly realized that's exactly what it was, an act. Zeb was genuine and unchanging, Eli was putting on a show, trying to be more than he actually was. In truth, he was a broken scared little boy, who missed his father. This made me initially put Eli out of my mind as incompatible, as he would never be able to

146

offer me anything that I wanted for my life.

Driving home I became aware that Eli was a very careful driver. He was rhythmic and in control of it. I said, "You at least drive very carefully."

"Yeah, of course I am. I got my baby sister on board. My mom would kill me if I let anything happen to her."

I looked over at Mae who was fast asleep leaning against the door. I imagine that another reason he was driving carefully was to prevent Mae from being woken up by a sharp turn or a hard bump. I smiled looking at Mae, she was super cute and she was incredibly bright for her age.

Eli dropped us off at the house and then drove off with a wave of his hand out the window. I smiled and leaned into Zeb as we walked towards the front door of our home.

"I had a good time, thank you for taking me. Now, tell me what you two were talking about when he wanted to talk to you alone in the bedroom."

"Well, he asked me if I loved you, and I said yes. Then he asked if we had sex, from which I said that I do not kiss and tell. He asked the typical boy questions about you, much of which I told him that it was none of his business."

"Like what? What did he ask that you told him none of his business about?"

"You know, he was asking how you felt, and the shape of your nipples. To be honest, it was all a little embarrassing and contrived. I don't know why he was asking me all that, it was almost like he was putting on a show."

"I see, well thank you for not telling him my secrets. I would not have been happy about you sharing that."

"I would never reveal anything about you, that you did not give me explicit permission to reveal."

"Thank you. Do you think everyone is in bed right now?"

We were still standing outside in front of the garage door. He stepped around and looked through the kitchen window to a dark house. It didn't look obvious that anyone was awake.

"I'm not sure, Clemmy is usually up, but she's probably just hanging out in her bedroom."

"Well…," I said suggestively, "do you want to, do *it* again?"

Zeb smiled, and slowly shook his head. "I do, but probably not tonight. It's late and I'm really tired. Plus, we both have to get up early tomorrow, me for school and you for a doctor's appointment."

"It's okay, I totally understand. I'll just have to take care of it myself," I said with a big hinting grin. He smiled back, then opened the door to the house, and went inside. Giving me a kiss, he took a right towards his bedroom, and I went left towards the den.

Lying on my bed I looked at my phone. I bet I could get Eli on *Snapchat*. It didn't take me but a few moments to locate Eli, his goofy face popping up. It helped that we exchanged numbers to get into a group text with Zeb, so we could all plan little outings. I sent him a snap of my face, with the words written in front of it: "Who knew I'd find your goofy ass on here?"

He snapped me back very quickly, a picture of his own face with the words written: "I did."

After the initial picture exchange, he sent his messages via text through the message part of the *Snapchat* app.

-Eli: Why are you messaging me this late at night, aren't you supposed to be with Zeb?

-Me: Well, he went to bed, I asked if he wanted to have sex and he said he was tired.

-Eli: That chump, I would have jumped all over that.

-Me: prove it.

-Eli: Yeah right, good joke.

-Me: Well, you know how things get sometimes. I'm going to bed, talk to you tomorrow!

-Eli: Good night.

Chapter 19
Cheat

Zeb woke me up before he went to school, he remembered I had a doctor's appointment and knew I would want to spend a little time getting dressed to the nine before going. I got up and hopped in the shower, afterwards getting dressed in a black revealing, provocative, and short dress. I also wore Clemmy's knee high boots and borrowed small Lulu Lemon cropped jacket to cover my arms.

I woke up thinking about Eli today, wondering if he was busy. I decided I'd send him a little snap of my outfit and see if he'd bite on my looks.

-Me: **Picture sent**

-Me: What do you think?

-Eli: WOW! Zeb is super lucky!

-Me: I'm going to a doctor's appointment, what are you doing today?

-Eli: Nothing much. Want to come over?

-Me: Sure, give me an address.

-Eli: My address is 17 Trail end Road.

-Eli: No one will be home; my mom is at her boyfriends and my siblings are all at school.

-Me: Good. I will see you after my doc appt.

Eli has changed the messages to delete after 1 minute

I thought to myself, 'This will be interesting. Are

you sure you want to do this? There's no going back after you do this.'

Nodding to myself, I applied the last little bit of makeup I needed, went into Zeb's room and grabbed one of the condoms that were hidden in a drawer. 'This is gonna be fine, no one ever has to know.'

I drove over to the clinic where my doctor appointment was being held. I had to get some blood tests drawn. My doctor wanted to recheck my lipids and triglycerides, because the last time they were incredibly high. Of course, they were, I didn't exercise, and I never planned on it. It didn't take long for my doctor appointment to be completed, and I went out and got in Clemmy's car.

The drive over to Eli's house was not very far. It only took me around ten minutes. Pulling into a very steep driveway, I saw a big deck out in front of the front door, and a one car carport on the side of the house. It was a cute little house, for being small and on the side of a mountain. Eli came out onto the front porch and stood there awkwardly as I eased up the drive.

"Hey, you really are incredibly sexy," Eli commented when I got out of the car and walked up the porch steps.

Beaming, I smiled at him and boldly walked up, grabbed him by his face and pulled him into a long sensual kiss. I could tell by the tightness growing in his pants that I had an effect on him. I don't know how long I should risk being gone, but I was going to use every minute of it.

Eli brought me inside his home, I noticed the concrete floors and a chaotic living room. There were toys everywhere, I assumed from his little brother and sisters. Eli grabbed my hand, "Come with me," and escorted me to a room that had a bunkbed in it.

Grinning, I said, "I am not doing it on a bunkbed."

"Uhh, oh! I got an idea, come with me."

Eli escorted me into a room with a single queen-sized bed in it, and women's clothes hanging in the closet. This was his mother's room. Good enough for me, I quickly slipped out of my clothes and sat on the bed.

With a big smile on his face, Eli asked, "Are you on birth control?"

I nodded, and as he climbed into the bed with me, he said, "Good, I don't like using condoms."

After completing several sessions, we both lay in the messy bed breathing hard. I decided I needed to check the time, I don't know how long I was here, but I felt like it was hours. I looked at my phone and noticed several missed calls and messages. It was 1:15 pm.

"Oh no!" I gasped, hurrying up and throwing my clothes on really quickly.

"What's the matter?"

"I will cut your balls off if you ever tell anyone what happened here."

"I won't I promise."

I looked at my phone and decided to read the messages.

-Clemmy: Hey, worried about you, you should have been home an hour ago. Everything okay?

-Clemmy: Tanna, it's been three hours since your doctor's appointment, I really need to know where you are. We are worried something happened to you.

-Parker: Hey Tanna, I just came by the doctor's office, you weren't there. This isn't okay for you to be taking off without letting us know where you were going. I'm going to need you to respond and be home in thirty minutes, that's 1:45 pm. If you're not, I'm going to have to start the search party.

-Clemmy: I'm going to call the cops in 30 minutes and report you as missing and my car as missing. Please let us know if you're okay.

-Zeb: Hey babe, my dad and Clemmy are freaking out because they can't get ahold of you. Are you okay?

I had 15 minutes to get home. I had 15 minutes to make sure I didn't look like I had been having sex for the last 3 hours. I ran outside to the car and responded to Parker first, then to Clemmy, then Zeb.

-Me to Parker: Hey sorry, one of my friends was about to hurt herself, so I rushed over to her house to help her.

-Parker: After everything, you should have known that all you had to do was shoot me or Clemmy a message letting us know that you were heading to a friend's house. We would have said OK. You need to get to the house immediately. I will talk to you when I get home.

-Me: Okay.

-Me to Clemmy: Hey sorry, one of my friends was about to hurt herself, so I rushed over to her house to help her. I'm really sorry, I will make it up to you guys by filling the car up with gas. Please forgive me.

-Clemmy: Get home, now.

-Me to Zeb: Hey, sorry for not responding, I was helping a friend out who was about to hurt herself, she was crying and called me, so I immediately went to her house.

-Zeb: Okay, no problem. I'm glad you're okay. I'll

see you when I get home.

Pulling into the house it was 1:52 pm. I went straight inside and explained to Clemmy what happened.

"So, my friend Beth was feeling very suicidal and called me. She said she had a knife to her wrists and was going to kill herself if I didn't get there to stop her. I went immediately to help her. I stayed with her until her mom got home. I didn't have my phone on me, I had left it in the car because I was in such a hurry."

"I understand. Please just be conscientious of the fact that we care about you and are worried about you. You know we are not that strict of parents, all you had to do was let me know and I would not have told you not to go. Please do better in the future."

"I will."

I sat on the couch for a little bit, then decided to go lay down in Zeb's room. As soon as I walked through his door and it shut behind me, I sighed with relief. My lies had worked. Clemmy believed me. I knew she would convince Parker as well. Zeb was super trusting and loved me unconditionally, so I wasn't worried about convincing him. It was all gravy baby.

-Me on *Snapchat:* Well, I made it home, no one is the wiser. They bought my lies.

-Eli on *Snapchat*: Good. That was fun, I definitely want to do that again.

-Me on *Snapchat*: Oh, we will, just have to figure out a time and place.

-Eli on *Snapchat*: I'm so glad you are on birth control.

-Me on *Snapchat*: Me too. I'm going to go get cleaned up, I got your juices running down my leg into these boots.

That evening, Zeb came home, gave me a hug and a kiss then got on his computer to play some games with his friend Austin. I had no complaints this time, I felt a little guilty about cheating on him with his cousin, but not that guilty. Zeb had no right to have as much as he did in life. I realized sitting there thinking about what happened, that I didn't recall when my goal of making Kyle jealous ceased being a goal, now it was all about preserving my freedom. Perhaps it will change again, I couldn't know.

A few minutes after six, Parker came home. He came straight to Zeb's room, looked at Zeb and said, "Zeb, I need you to go to the other room for a little while, I need to talk to Tanna."

After Zeb got up and left the room, Parker sat down at the desk and rotated the chair to look at me directly. He was furious, I could tell by the way his eyes bore into me. I don't think he believed me, and after he spoke, I knew he didn't.

"I'm going to be very honest with you right now, I'm going to give you the 3rd degree." He took a deep breath. "Tanna, I don't know where you went today after your doctor's appointment, but I don't believe for one second you went to a girls house who was needing mental health support."

"I was," I lied.

"How old is this girl?"

"She's eighteen."

"Is she in school?"

"No, she graduated last year."

"Why didn't you call her mom?"

"I did, I waited until her mom got there."

"Show me the messages and call log."

"I called her mom on her phone; I didn't have the number. The messages automatically delete because they are on *Snapchat*."

"Convenient. Here's what I think, I think you were with a boy. I think you were with a boy the entire time you were gone. I don't believe for one second that you're telling the truth."

"You think I would cheat on Zeb?" I started the fake waterworks, tearing up.

"Yes, I do. I can't prove it, yet, but I do think that. No teenager would go that long without checking their phone at least once. I don't think your little face time friends are all innocent either. I think that Lucky guy you face time practically every day, is more than a friend."

"Lucky is fifteen."

"And? Fifteen-year-olds get crushes too. Even if you're not into him, he's definitely into you. So, you're either leading him on, or you are in on it too. I can't prove which yet."

"I can't believe you would think I would cheat on Zeb!"

"I really do. I want you to know something, I don't trust you, I think you're lying and cheating. I feel it in my gut that you are. My gut doesn't lead me wrong. I can't prove it yet, but know that I will find out, eventually."

Parker left the room before I could form another lie to try to get him to believe. I'm going to have to cut back on face timing the guys while Parker is home. I'm also going to have to find other ways to do what I want to do with him watching so much. I'll figure it out. I glowered at the door that swung shut behind Parker. Why are there always obstacles in my way?

Chapter 20
Sneaking

At school, the next day I was sick to my stomach. I didn't want to be there, I was failing three classes, and I felt like everyone was looking at me funny, like they knew my secret. It wasn't the first time I had cheated on Zeb, but it was the first time I had any sort of physical interaction with someone other than Zeb, since he and I said we loved each other.

The more I thought about Zeb, the more I realized I actually did love him. He was sweet and goal oriented. It made me sick to my stomach to think about what I was doing, having sex with his cousin. Is that the kind of person I am? I didn't know, I'm sure time would tell.

I vomited after breakfast. The nurse wouldn't believe me if I just told her I was sick, so I took a picture of my vomit and marched to the nurse's office.

"I'm sick, I need to go home. Can you please call my mom and tell her to come get me?"

"Tanna, we have gone over this, if you're not running a fever or actively throwing up, we aren't going to call your parents."

"I did just actively throw up, look, I took a picture." I held my phone up so the nurse could see. I was glaring at her, how could she hold my own health against me like that, it was 'actively' rude. The nurse quickly glanced at my phone, rolled her eyes, then told me to sit down so she could take my temperature.

"Well, you're not running a fever. Stay here, I will go call your mom."

"Please call my dad, not my mom. My mom doesn't believe anything I say."

"I will call who is on your contact list Tanna, I can't change the rules."

After sitting in the nurse's office for twenty minutes, the nurse finally came back in and said, "Your mom insists that you're fine. She asked if you were running a fever, which I told her you were not."

"I'm SICK!! I CAN'T BE HERE ANYMORE!" I screamed at the nurse, then stormed out of her office. I had to go back to class. I would have tried to urge Clemmy to finish the guardianship paperwork, the sooner the better. My mom was ridiculous.

Back in class I sat there thinking about Eli and Zeb. I did enjoy my time with Eli, but I didn't care for him. I knew if I was with him, we would end up cheating on each other all the time. I would be dammed if someone cheated on me. That's just now how this works.

-Me on *Snapchat*: Eli, what are you doing?

-Eli on *Snapchat*: Nothin, just chillin at the house.

-Me on *Snapchat*: Want to hang tomorrow night? I think I found a way out of the house.

-Eli on *Snapchat*: Sure, how you going to do that without Uncle Parker finding out? He has cameras on all the doors and all over the house.

-Me on *Snapchat*: Because I can turn the garage door camera towards the wall today. If they don't fix it, I will know they aren't watching it all that much.

The cats are always in and out of the garage, so I assume their notifications are muted, otherwise they would be going off ALL the time.

-Eli on *Snapchat*: Sounds good for me, keep me updated.

-Me on *Snapchat*: Will do.

I smirked. I guess I don't feel so guilty about cheating on Zeb after all. I mean, if he's not going to give me what I want, I'm going to have to get it from somewhere. I have needs too. I'm a free spirit, no one will ever be able to cage me.

I started feeling better, not as nauseous. I had an hour left at school before I had to meet Parker by Juan Pepe's for a ride home. It was always by the restaurant because there were so many students at the school, it would take over an hour to get through the pickup line.

Parker and I got to the house around 3:15 pm. I went inside and put my book bag down, I could tell that he didn't trust me in the least. He would constantly be cutting his eyes at me when I got on my phone. I would have to be careful with what I looked at and where I was looking while I was at the house.

When Clemmy got home I quickly went to her and threw all my woes at her. "Clem! Today was absolutely miserable. I was so sick; I was throwing up during every period. I went to the nurse and had her call my mom. That witch told me I was faking it and had to go back to class. I even took a picture of my vomit. They still didn't believe me. It was the worst! Sometimes life just sucks!"

"Oh sweetheart, I'm so sorry you had to deal with that today. Are you feeling better now?"

"Yeah I'm feeling better now, it's just at school I

feel super sick."

"Hmm, I wonder if you are having anxiety attacks and that's what's causing you to feel nauseous."

Parker chimed in, "I bet that's exactly what it is. You have a lot of stress at school, and with the stunt your mom pulled last week, I imagine you aren't feeling good at all while you're there. Don't you have an anxiety medication you're supposed to be taking?"

"Yes, I do… I just haven't been wanting to take that kind of stuff."

"Sweetheart, I totally understand that, but the doctors gave you the medicine to help you. It's an as-needed medicine, so if you don't need it, don't take it, but vice versa, if you do need it, take it."

"Okay, I'll give it a try. Do you think there's anything else I can do?"

"Yes, I'll go to the store and buy you some anti-nausea candies, they are over the counter and usually for pregnant women. The sour nature of the candies or ginger in them will help you feel less nauseated. If you're still feeling sickly after that, I will see about calling your mom and getting her to do something, until we can get guardianship of you."

"When are we going to do the paperwork for that?"

"Well, your mom and dad got their side done, I just have to have a day where I'm not working as late as I have been, and we can take it to a notary and have it done. I got a friend who is a notary-public that I think can meet us to do it after hours if need be."

"Okay thank you."

That evening after Zeb had gotten home, we were lying in his bedroom. The room was becoming increasingly discombobulated the longer that I had been here. It was completely trashed where I kept my stuff, but I ignored it. Every now and then Zeb would make a small comment about how it was getting pretty dirty in his room. I would just chuckle and nod.

When it was close to the time, I had to leave Zeb's room, I knew that Parker and Clemmy had gone to bed, they both had to work the next day. I rolled over on my stomach, looking intently at Zeb, I was going to come onto him and see if he rejected me. He was asleep, he had fallen asleep during the show. I knew I should have picked one that wasn't so boring. I thought that it was possible he was faking it, but decided I wouldn't push it tonight. I wanted to test my theory on the camera that looked at the garage side door.

I snuck out into the garage and turned the camera. I made sure not to get in the range of view. After turning the camera, I walked out the side door and stood in the crisp, cool, December air. It was quiet outside, other than the soft rustle of dead leaves, and the occasional swoosh of a car passing on a distant road, it was as silent as roadkill. I stood there for a while, then went around back and sat in one of the yard chairs. The neighborhood cat came slinking up towards me, and I didn't move. I stared at it, it stared at me. This cat was a huge black and white female. Her name was Hermana. She belonged to a Latin American family that lived next door. She usually did not allow anyone but her tribe to pet and love on her, yet she came right up to me and flopped her jiggling body over on her back.

After sitting outside for twenty minutes loving on Hermana, I got up and went back in through the garage door. The house was as still as an unconscious prostitute who was beaten nearly to death by her client. I smiled. I crawled into bed and pulled out my phone, shooting a quick snap to Eli.

-Me on *Snapchat*: Plan works, my sneaking paid off. Will holler at you tomorrow.

-Eli on Snapchat: K.

Chapter 21
The Library

Waking up the next day was a chore. I was groggy and feeling very unrested. I rubbed the goo out of my eyes and stretched as best as I could. The thunderstorms going on outside didn't help with making me want to get up. With all the different things going on around the house, I wasn't going to be able to sleep anyway. Parker had already gone to work; Zeb was up and getting some breakfast with his little brother. Clemmy was making her coffee and getting her workstation prepared because she had to work from home. I was excited because today, I should be able to get my car. It would have to be after school, but at least with Clemmy working from home, I wouldn't have to ride on Zeb's motorcycle in the rain. Zeb would drive me to school in Clemmy's car. It was going to be a good day.

The second I got to school I began to feel nauseous again. It had to be anxiety. What was I so nervous and scared about? I thought about it, and it occurred to me that because I was failing three classes, they may call me in to go to summer school, and I didn't want that to happen. I hated school, I was never planning on going to any college or doing anything after I graduated. I was going to get married and lounge around all day, every day.

I decided that I was going to break my promise to myself of never putting any more chemicals in my body. I was going to take my anti-anxiety pill. Popping the top off the medicine container, I quickly extracted one of the small blue pills and threw it in my mouth. I had been taking pills for so many years of my life, I didn't even need water to swallow them. Down the hatch they went.

After fifteen minutes, my nausea started to subside, leaving me frustrated that Clemmy was correct about me just having anxiety. I still didn't want to be at school so I'm going to call my dad. I bet he would take me to the doctor if I asked him to.

When my dad answered the phone he said, "Hello?"

"Daddy… I don't feel good, can you come get me and take me to the doctor?"

"What's the matter honey?"

"I'm just really sick to my stomach, and my nose is runny. I just can't be at school right now, can you take me to the doctor?"

"Sure honey, I'll be there soon, go to the nurse's office and wait for me."

"Thank you so much, I love you."

"I love you too, see you soon Tanna."

I went to the nurse's office and told her that I wasn't feeling well, and that my dad was going to come pick me up and take me to the doctor. She nodded and told me to sit in the front office chairs until he got there. Mumbling under my breath, "Stupid bitch." I sat down in the chairs by the front office and waited.

"Hey honey-bear, you ready to go? You got all your stuff? Your mom already called the clinic and checked you in, we are going to go straight there."

"Hi daddy, yes, I got all my stuff. Thank you for coming to get me."

As we got in the car and pulled away from the school my dad gave me a small side-eye and asked me cautiously, "Are you pregnant honey-bear?"

I gasped and put my hand flat on my chest, as if offended, "Dad! Of course not! I'm not pregnant!"

"Well, your mom said you didn't fill your birth control since October and that you were living with a boy. I was just worried is all."

"I would have to have had sex to get pregnant dad, dang."

"That's a relief to hear honey-bear."

We got to the clinic and went inside. After seeing the doctor, they surmised that I had nothing wrong with me. That it was possible my diet that consisted of too many fatty foods was causing me to be nauseated. It was recommended that I cut back on the bad foods and go on a BRAT diet. That is Banana's, Rice, Applesauce, and Toast. I was most definitely not going to do that, but I would say I would just to appease them.

My dad took me back to Zeb's house and dropped me off.

"I love you hon! Get some rest and start feeling better, okay? I missed you."

"I love and missed you too daddy! Bye!"

My dad left as I walked through the front door. Clemmy was lying down on the couch taking a nap, it was her lunch hour at work. I thought it was incredibly sensible that she would take a nap during her lunch hour, as it probably allowed her to be more alert and process her job better. I decided I would call the place where my car was and see if I was good to come get it today.

"Hello, Turkis Auto Repair how can I help you?"

"Hi, this is Tanna Parmstring, is my car ready to be picked up?"

"Hey there Ms. Parmstring, yes, your car is available for pick up anytime today between now and two thirty. We close a little early today because of an employee awards ceremony."

"What time do you open tomorrow?"

"We open up at 8 am tomorrow morning, you can pick up anytime between 8 am and 4 pm tomorrow."

"Thank you, I'll see you tomorrow."

Bummed because I knew that I wouldn't have time to go get my car today after they told me what time they were closing. Clemmy didn't get off work until 4:30, but maybe I could convince her to take me to my car tomorrow before she had to work at 8 am. Even if she dropped me off and let me wait there until they opened, I'd be okay with that too.

"Hey Tanna, you're home early, what's the matter?"

"My dad came and got me from school today, to take me to the doctor. I wasn't feeling well, even with the sour ginger candies and the anxiety pills."

"Oh, honey I'm so sorry, I know what it's like being sick all the time. What did the doctor say?"

"They said I was eating too many fatty foods, and to go on a BRAT diet. My stupid dad even asked me if I was pregnant! Can you believe that!?"

"Wow, that's kind of a jerk thing to ask. As for the BRAT diet, we can make that happen, I'll head to the store after work and get you the things you need. We already have rice and bananas and toast; I'll grab some applesauce. Do you need me to make you some rice and toast?"

"No, I'll be okay, I'm not hungry right now," I lied; I was starving right now. I just didn't want to eat rice and toast.

"Okay, no problem, just let me know if you need anything."

"Actually, there is one thing, I have to go pick up my car today before 2 pm, do you think that's possible? If not, it has to be between 8 am and 4 pm tomorrow."

"It's going to have to be tomorrow, I have a lot of work to do before 4:30 today, but tomorrow I'm off because I have a doctor's appointment at 11 in Little Rock."

"Great, tomorrow it is."

"We will go get your car first thing in the morning, then head to Little Rock together and have a girl's day."

"That sounds like a lot of fun!" I lied again, I wanted to go see Eli, but I wasn't going to tell her that.

"You know Eli and Zeb were talking the other day about going to Little Rock to do some big arcade there. That would have been fun. Eli is always goofing off and being silly when he and Zeb hang out."

"Oh yeah?" Clemmy asked, looking at me oddly.

"Yeah… Okay I'm going to let you get back to work, I'm going to go lay down for a little while until I feel better. Love you Clem."

"Love you too Tanna."

I went to the bedroom kicking myself, why did I even have to bring up Eli? That made no sense, just out of the blue and random like that. I got to be smarter if I'm going to continue to fool these people. I haven't checked my group messenger in a long time, but I didn't feel like I wanted to right now anyway. I wanted to talk to Eli.

-Me on *Snapchat*: Hey. Wyd.

-Eli on *Snapchat*: nm. What's the plan for tonight?

-Me on *Snapchat*: I'm going to rock your world.

-Eli on *Snapchat*: I can't wait. You rocked it the last time that's for sure. So many times, too!

-Me on *Snapchat*: Try to last longer than 30 seconds each time this time. I hate having to wait for you to get ready again.

-Eli on *Snapchat*: You should take that as a compliment!

-Me on *Snapchat*: Here's the deal, this has to be nothing but a friend with benefits type of thing. No attachment, no emotion, just sex. Do you understand?

-Eli on *Snapchat*: You sure you can stop yourself from falling in love with me?

-Me on *Snapchat*: Obviously. You're not my type.

-Eli on *Snapchat*: Ouch. Well, you're definitely my type, but I'll control myself.

-Me on *Snapchat*: Pick me up at midnight, on the corner of the street.

-Eli on *Snapchat*: I'll be there.

When Zeb got home from work, he came to me and hugged me. I didn't have to ask for a hug, he just threw his arms around me and pulled me in close. Looking up at him, I asked, "What's this for?"

"I just love you. Thank you for being understanding about my issues with physical contact. I wish I could change it."

"I love you too Zeb. You're the best thing that's ever happened to me, you make me so happy."

"Let's go hang out with Eli tonight, he wants to go

bowling and get some Nachos."

"Eli? How about I go with you guys, but you two bowl, I'll just hang out."

"Works for me."

We went to the bowling alley, meeting Eli there. It was just as Zeb had planned, he and Eli played a few games of Bowling and I sat there and just cheered and laughed as the two of them goofed off. Zeb was silly, and Eli tried to match his energy of silliness. Zeb would break into dancing when certain songs came on, then sing at the top of his lungs on the chorus's he knew. It was really charming and funny. His smile was bright and reached his eyes. He really did love Elisha. This was his best friend, his most reliable confidant, and his biggest betrayer. I thought for a moment what would happen to Zeb if he found out that his cousin was sowing his seeds inside me. I got a sick sense of satisfaction when I thought about the level of broken it would make Zeb. His entire being would be destroyed. I suddenly realized that no matter what happened, I would be satisfied. Did my new goal in life become breaking this man? Did my new goal in life evolve to that level of sickness? Is my sense of self awareness that perfect that I can tell that about myself? 'Yes,' I thought, 'Yes it is.'

After we got home, Zeb beckoned me to his room. Everyone in the house had already gone to bed, so I had an idea of what was going to happen.

"I have to run to the bathroom really quick. Give me a second, I'll be right there, I promise," I said with a quick kiss.

I got to the bathroom and quickly pulled my phone out, it was a little after ten thirty. I shot Eli a quick

Snap.

-Me on *Snapchat:* Just an update, unless I message you again, don't show up.

-Eli on *Snapchat*: Wait why?

I left him on read. I quickly cleaned myself up and let off a little gas, then put on a little perfume and went to Zeb. He was lying on the bed, waiting for me. I smiled and joined him, quickly slipping out of my clothing.

Loving Zeb was a far cry different than Eli. It was more tender, where Eli was more "wham bam thank you ma'am" style. When Zeb and I were finished, he quickly fell asleep, I was beginning to nod off too before I had an intense stomach cramp. I got up and went to the bathroom, figuring it to be gas, which I refused to pass in front of Zeb.

Sitting on the toilet I decided I was awake now and it was only 11:45 pm. I decided I'd shoot Eli a snap and have some more fun tonight.

-Me on Snapchat: Come get me.

-Eli on Snapchat: On my way.

I cleaned myself up and snuck out of the bathroom, heading towards the den. No one was awake in the house but me and three playful cats. I went into the garage, peaking around the corner and checking to make sure the camera was still turned towards the wall. It wasn't. Someone had come and turned the camera back around. Frowning, I decided to take a chance. I grabbed a broom that was leaning against the wall, reached around and knocked the camera to the side. I got lucky with the roll as it rolled facing the wall.

Grinning, I whispered to myself, "Must be meant to be."

At the corner of the street, I saw Eli's little white car sitting there, waiting for me. I walked over and opened the passenger door. I looked at Eli and smiled. "Hey lover, what are you doing out here in the middle of the night? Wanna party?"

He laughed and said, "I was going to say that exact same thing!"

"Let's go find a dark alley somewhere."

We pulled out onto the road and started looking around for a spot to park and set up at. Our first thought was going to Lorell park, but as we pulled into the parking lot, we noticed there was a lot of light there. We also noticed a couple of cops sitting there chit chatting. That wasn't going to work, so we pulled back out on the highway and pressed on through the town. We swung by the grocery store that was closed, but again there were a lot of lights and what appeared to be homeless people walking around the parking lot.

Finally, after driving around for nearly an hour, we found the public library. It was set off near a small forest, with a bunch of decorative trees planted all through the parking lot. The back corner near the dumpsters was super dark. It was the perfect spot for some nighttime shenanigans.

"Finally," I muttered.

"I know right, I was about to ask for road head if we didn't find something sooner."

"You're disgusting. I'm not putting that in my mouth."

"You've done it before."

I stared at him for a moment. "Just take your clothes off. Hurry up."

Once again, we didn't use a condom. I wasn't too

worried, it had only been a month since I took my birth control, so I thought wasn't at any risk of getting pregnant right now. Even if I did, I would just say it was Zeb's which would lock me in his family forever.

"I think I like this spot, next time we don't have to drive around for so long, so we can do it more than once, and not have to hurry back."

I looked at him and considered his words, it was a good point. Nodding I said, "Yes, I think I like the library a lot too. Take me back to the house."

When we got back to the house, I snuck back in the side door, not looking back once at him as he pulled away. No one was awake. It was quiet and still. I smiled, knowing no one would ever know or find out about my secret adventure at the library. I am beginning to really love this freedom.

Chapter 22
The Weeks to Christmas

The next few days seemed to pass incredibly fast. I went and got my car without issue, and with it being the weekend, I was only able to sneak out of the house one other time, to go with Eli to the library. Everyone thought I was sick, because I kept sleeping and snoozing during the day. That tends to happen when one stays out and about all night a couple nights in a row. The pressure of being a part of a loving family and me being tired all the time really started to get to me. I needed a small break from the house, Parker's side-eye, and Zeb's curious concern about my health. I would have to get out of the house for a little while after school today.

Today was Monday, I got to school and struggled with my anxiety again. I was nauseous and on the verge of vomiting through my first hour of classes. My face was flushed and my mouth watering, I knew it was a matter of seconds before I spewed my waffle all over the floor of my English class. I got up and ran from the classroom, not saying a word to the teacher.

-Me: Mom, I'm very, very, sick. I really need you to come get me.

-Me: Clemmy, can you please try to get ahold of my mom, I'm throwing up everywhere again. I can barely function. I just can't be here anymore.

-Clemmy: I'll see what I can do sweetheart. Take one of those sour candies, and maybe an anxiety pill.

-Me: I already did. It's not working.

I had not taken anything even though I said I had, but I decided while I sat there that I would. I just didn't understand why I was so anxious and stressed at school. I waited outside the nurse's office for the rest of my second period, realizing I wasn't going to be getting a text back from my mom, I stormed to my third period class.

After school that day, I got home and complained to Clemmy about how I hated being at school sick. I felt like it was every day, and there was nothing anyone or anything could do to stop it.

"I need a break from everything, do you think I can go hang out with Ruthelle for a little while? I'm sorry, I just want to be away right now."

"Sure, be back before nine tonight."

"Thank you."

Zeb wasn't even home from work yet. Since I was already dressed from school, I didn't change anything about what I was wearing. I simply grabbed my car keys and went to Ruthelle's. When I got there, Ruthelle and her mom were sitting on the porch.

"Hey there Tanna, how are you doing?"

"Hey Ms. Craine, I'm doing okay, how about you?"

"Fair to middling child. Fair to middling."

"Hey Ruthelle, can we go to your room and talk for a little while? I need to vent a little."

"Sure babe, let's go."

Ruthelle and I went to her solar system of a room and laid down on top of the covers together. We both stared up at the slowly dimming and brightening lights that spattered her ceiling.

"So, I started seeing Zeb's cousin at night."

"WHAT!?" Ruthelle quickly sat up, staring at me.

"Yeah, we just hit it off and I started sneaking out at night and meeting him. He's a couple years older than me."

"Girl, what happens if Zeb finds out?"

"I'll probably get kicked out. Besides, I'm only with Zeb because I have to keep up appearances, so I don't get kicked out of the house."

"That seems off to me. Why would they invite you to their vacation if they were going to kick you out if you and Zeb broke up?"

"Because I think they only invited me because of Zeb."

"Why in the world did you start sleeping with… what's his name?"

"His name is Eli. Girl, I was so tired of being neglected by Zeb, and ignored all the time. Every single day he ignores me. Then Eli came around and came on to me, so I slurped it right up." The lies rolled smoothly off my tongue.

"Dang, I don't know what to say to all that."

We sat there for a little while, in silence. Finally, Ruthelle said, "You know my brother has a crush on you, you're a little older, but you could have given him a shot, instead of someone Zeb knew."

"Eww, he's a child."

"Yeah, that's true."

We hung out for a little while longer before I decided that I had been there long enough. I decided to go home, maybe I could hang out with Zeb for a little while before we had to go to bed. If he chose to ignore me, I would be going to see Eli tonight, though if I'm being honest, I'd probably go see Eli regardless of how Zeb treated me.

This sort of thing went on for what seemed like every day for two weeks. Each day I would go to school, feel sick and complain to my mom to no avail. I would then go home and hang out with Zeb. Most days he gave me attention and showered me with love. Also, truth be told, after I went to bed, I still went to see Eli.

It was a week from Christmas now, and I had to go do a little shopping for Parker, Clemmy, and Des. I spent most of my meager funds on myself, and junk food. I had ordered a small blanket that said, "Tanna loves Zeb." I loved it, because not only did it display loudly and proudly that I loved Zeb, but it also helped set the precedent for my ownership of Zeb. If he used the blanket or had it on display, everyone who saw it would know that he was taken by me.

I wasn't going to buy Eli anything for Christmas. He was still just a friend; we just had a lot of fun together. I could tell he was falling for me; I could tell that he wanted to be more than friends. Tonight, sitting naked in his car with the bright full moon light shining through the windows, he confirmed my beliefs.

"I want you to break up with Zeb and be mine."

"What? Are you kidding me?"

"I'm serious. You could come live with me, we can get a place together, both of us work, and just be happy and in love."

"Eli, no. I don't want to be with you. I don't want to be anything more than friends with benefits with you. This has gone on long enough, please take me home. I won't be having you come get me anymore. Plus, Emma and her girlfriend are coming to Arkansas soon, so I won't be able to leave the house anyway."

"Tanna please. I love you…" Eli began to ugly cry, tears streaking down his face.

I looked at him in disgust. "I don't love you, Eli. You're pathetic. You will never get a girl to love you. What kind of friend and family are you? Seducing your best friend's girlfriend?" I was on a roll, enjoying the turmoil he was being put through. I reveled in his discomfort and pain as every word I said to him struck him across the face like a slap. "You are nothing, you undersized child. You couldn't even satisfy me once. I would never choose to be with someone like you."

We drove back to the house; the only sounds were the road and his sniffling as he quietly wept. I may have been a little extra cruel to him, but I didn't care. It made me feel something that was a better feeling than any I had felt my entire life. I felt powerful.

Chapter 23
The Perfect Relationship

We were released from school early for Christmas break today, and when I got home, Parker was already there. "Hey Tanna, how was your day?"

"Not terrible, I didn't feel sick today, which was a relief."

"Good to hear. Look, so we are looking at the sleeping arrangements for tomorrow, Emma and Payton are coming out to visit for Christmas, they'll go home after the new year. I'm going to place a bed in Zeb's room, next to his bed. Are you going to be okay sleeping in the room with him? Not sharing a bed of course."

"That would be great, can we put the bed next to the side he sleeps on, so I can hold his hand as I fall asleep?"

"We can put the bed on either side, it makes no difference to me. I'll expect the door to be left open, and you two to respect each other."

"Absolutely."

"Good, I've already discussed it with Zeb, he is okay with it as long as you were. He values your opinion and respects the woman you are."

"That's really sweet. Where are Emma and Payton going to sleep?"

"They are going to sleep in Des's room, and he's

going to sleep in the den."

"It's going to be a full house. What are you going to do now that you're going to be outnumbered by girls in the house?"

"Nah, it'll be fine, there's still more guys. We got, the three boy cats too."

"That's just cheating."

"The truth hurts sometimes."

The next day Parker cut out really early to go get Emma and Payton. I was very concerned about having the two extra girls in the house. I would have to share the attention of everyone, and Emma was so intimidating. I wondered if Payton was just as intimidating or if she was going to be normal.

I didn't wake up until almost noon today, my body is still trying to recover from weeks of staying up all night and most of each day. When I got out of bed, Clemmy was up and about straightening up some of her Christmas decorations.

"Good morning Clemmy, do you need help with anything?"

"Good morning sleepyhead, sure, grab that right there and pin it up here."

We worked for about an hour, putting the final details on her decorations. We had about thirty minutes until Emma and Payton made it to the house. The closer it gets to them being here the more nervous and anxious I felt. I had a gut-wrenching feeling that these two girls would be a complete game changer for my tiny little paradise I'd built with this family.

When Parker pulled into the drive, I sat on the couch and waited for them to come in. Clemmy hopped up and rushed to the door, followed by Des. Everyone was excited to see the girls, except me. I'm sure Zeb would have been jumping up and down to see them too, except that he was at work. This made me feel a little lonely and scared.

When the beautiful tall strawberry blonde Emma walked through the door, she was smiling from ear to ear. She reached back and grabbed the hand of another beautiful girl, I assumed this was Payton. Payton was very beautiful, taller than me but not nearly as tall as Emma. She had a similar eye color to Emma, just a little lighter blue. Her eyes contrasted well with her short dark brown hair, and her gorgeous thick eyelashes really made the blue pop. Her eyelashes were so long they curved up naturally, unlike mine which were short and straight like boar's hair. Jealousy flooded my heart as I looked at her, her teeth were straight and white, and she had a bright friendly smile as she walked through the door of the house. Her body wasn't thin, but I could tell she wasn't fat like me, she was athletic. Her legs looked incredibly powerful, which sent a small shiver of fear down my spine. I just hope she isn't as observant as Emma and Parker.

"Hey Tanna! How are you!? This is Payton, Payton this is Tanna."

"Hey Tanna, nice to meet you." Payton had a huskier voice, it was almost like a sultry Russian voice, with an American accent. I was immediately attracted to her even more. My attraction quickly came crashing down when I looked at Emma, who was eyeing me suspiciously. I felt like a hyena invading a lioness' territory.

"Hi Emma, Hi Payton, nice to meet you."

Emma grabbed Payton's hand and pulled her

towards the bedroom. "Come check out our room." Des was hot on their heels, not letting them run off without giving him a hug and him showing out a little. Little brothers were always acting silly.

After making their rounds, the two beautiful girls came into the living room and sat down on the couch next to me. Emma was animatedly chatting with Payton about something to do with a video game.

"My dad bought the new Spider-man Payti! I told him it was one of your favorite games, so he bought it, and got it downloaded on his PS5."

"Oooh that's awesome. When can I play it?"

"Now. He doesn't care, just play it whenever."

As the girls set up the game, I decided I didn't want to hang out in here anymore, so I got up and went to the bedroom. I lay down on my little bed next to Zeb's and tried to take a nap. I tossed back and forth, before slamming my fist into the bed, I picked up my phone and decided to check my messages.

-Lucky on Group Messenger: Hey, I haven't heard from you in a long time, everything okay?

-Lucky on Group Messenger: Well, I guess I'll catch you later, since you're clearly doing something else, I guess I'm just going to bounce.

-Kyle on text: Hey, long time no speak, what are you up to? Just been thinking about you lately, I miss you. I wanted to see if you wanted to get back together, just dump that dude and come be with me.

-Kyle on text: Well, I can clearly see I'm being ignored. It was worth a shot.

-JP on text: Hey girl wyd?

I decided to respond back to JP, he was my longtime crush, so maybe his parents would finally let him do something.

-Me on text: nm, what about you?

-Me on text: Your parents letting you date yet?

-JP on text: No, they said I can't date until I'm 16, and since that's only nine months away, lol.

Me on text: I'll be waiting. Lol

-JP on text: good.

Emma came to the door and knocked lightly. She stuck her head inside the room and said, "Whoa, this room is disgusting. Do you guys ever clean it?"

She crinkled her nose a little, looked around one more time then said, "Payton and I are going to go get some Starbuck's, you want to go?"

"Sure!"

I hopped out of bed and hurriedly grabbed my purse and went into the living room. I had noticed that Emma had grabbed her dad's keys and was urging Payton to save her game so we could leave.

Zeb got home a little while after we returned from the coffee shop. He greeted Emma and Payton, and then quickly hopped in the shower. It was necessary that he got a shower because he was dealing with wheelchairs again tonight, and they always made him smell disgusting. I was not about to let him lay next to me smelling like that.

That night, we went to bed, and I fell asleep with my hand up on his bed. I had nightmares that night, vivid and terrifying. I couldn't remember what they consisted of, I just jarred myself awake in the middle of the night. I felt off, sick to my stomach and simply weird.

I got up the next day and rushed to the bathroom vomiting and shaking. What was wrong with me? I've been throwing up and feeling nauseous almost every morning now for a week. Maybe Ruthelle would know, I would swing by there and ask her today.

After getting permission to go to Ruthelle's house, I showed up and quickly rushed into her room. She was laid up in bed still, being that it was only nine in the morning. I jumped on her bed. "Hey, get up. What are you doing still sleeping?"

Ruthelle groaned, "Ugh what are you doing here? I was up studying all night."

"I have an emergency; I need your help."

"What is the matter? Is someone hurt?"

"No… I think I might be pregnant."

"What! How!? I mean I know how, but didn't you use protection? Aren't you on birth control?"

"No Eli and I didn't use protection, and yes, I'm on birth control, at least I was in October. That's the last time I took my birth control, but it shouldn't have worn off already, right?"

"Girl… no, that's not how it works. First of all, if you miss one day of birth control, you run the risk of it not being effective at all, let alone two whole months. Second of all, what kind of dumbass doesn't wrap his dick before he sticks it in someone and blows his load. Don't tell me you let him nut inside you?"

I stared at her and asked softly my eyes brimming with tears, "What do I do?"

"First thing is we go get a pregnancy test and see. If you are, then we will discuss it afterwards, but for now, let's just hope you're not and are just coming down with a winter bug."

We went to the store and grabbed a couple of pregnancy tests, then headed back to her house. I didn't know how to take one of these, so I had Ruthelle show me.

Positive.

I cried. How could I be pregnant, what was I going to do? I would tell them it was Zeb's, then I would be free and clear... except he and I hadn't had sex in a few weeks, so if they could tell when the baby was conceived, he would know it wasn't his.

"Okay, okay, shh, shh, I got you." Ruthelle grabbed me in a warm embrace and held me close.

"Tanna, listen to me, I got an idea. Last year, I got pregnant, but I wasn't about to let a teen pregnancy ruin my chance at NASA. My mom took me to the clinic, and she got me these pills. The very day I was supposed to take them, I wound up having a miscarriage, so I didn't use them. They are called: Mifepristone. It's an abortion pill. You take one today, and one tonight. Tomorrow you will lose your child. It will look like you're having a really heavy period."

I thought about it for a second, this would work. No one would be the wiser. I can just explain that I'm having a particularly tough period. After coming to that realization, I dried up my tears really quickly.

"Thank you, Ruthie. You're the best friend a person could ever ask for."

"Of course, babe, I love you. You're my best friend."

I took one of the pills immediately, then I hopped back in my car and went back home. The sour feeling in my stomach continued to grow until it was almost painful. This was going to be a rough night, but I would survive it.

My stomach twisted and turned in the middle of the night, I felt the blood gushing out of the sides of my panties. Zeb was asleep. I cried, keeping my noise down to a minimum, I refused to give in and call out. The pain of this ordeal was almost unbearable. I lay curled up in the fetal position, as the life of the unborn child inside of me was extinguished. I almost allowed myself to consider who that child would have been, what they would become, and I squashed those thoughts with a cold-hearted determination. I would NOT feel bad for my own choices, I made the best choice for me, at the time.

I used another pair of underwear to sop up the blood and stashed the disgusting biohazard away in the bottom of the closet, beneath a layer of trash and dirty laundry.

I woke up the next day still feeling ill, but I wasn't in as much pain today. It was tolerable. I could deal with a little pain, I could play it off like I was just having period cramps. I grabbed a pad from the hallway and put it on my underwear, just in case I had any lasting bleeding. The day went fairly quickly, as I stayed to myself in my own private misery. I would see how Emma and Payton acted towards each other, loving and caring. They really did have the perfect relationship. They goofed off and played as much as they snuggled and loved one another. I was jealous that Emma and Payton would snuggle all the time, absolutely devoted to each other.

I hoped one day that Zeb and I could get to that level; I was afraid we wouldn't be able to. Our relationship was forced past the level of speed we should have been at, by me moving in with him. I knew it was what I was pushing for, so I could get his level of freedom and trust, but seeing how pure and amazing a perfect relationship could be, it made me think the age-old question of, "What if?"

Chapter 24
Christmas

Christmas Eve was upon us before any of us even expected it. We knew it was coming, it was just a surprise that it was actually here. That evening we sat around the couch, I was feeling a thousand percent better, everyone was happy. We all had hot cocoa in our hands, and were enjoying watching Clemmy's favorite Christmas movie, *Elf*.

As soon as the movie was over, Parker stood up, stretched his tall body, and said, "Alright everyone, time for bed. Santa's got to put out the gifts so he can get some sleep tonight too."

Des said with a laugh as he headed for bed, "Bye Buddies, I hope you find your dad."

Laughing, everyone got up excitedly chittering with one another as they headed towards their respective rooms. Each child knew that Santa in this case, meant Parker. Des was the last one to believe in a magical being that teleported into homes through their chimneys to leave candy and presents. He figured out the truth on his own a couple of Christmas's ago.

When the kids were safely tucked away into their bedrooms, Parker and Clemmy brought out the many gifts they had been wrapping and storing in their rooms for the last couple of weeks. The stockings were filled, the presents organized, and the cats were in heaven.

They thought all the new packages were a new playground for them to bounce around on and play chase.

Christmas morning brought a slew of happy children, chomping at the bit to get their gifts. This family had a different way of doing gift unwrapping than what I was used to at my parent's house. At my parents' house, we would just get up and open up everything with our name on it. Usually, it was three to four expensive gifts. At the Fowlers, we all ate breakfast first, then everyone was assigned a seat on the very large sectional couch. After everyone got situated, Parker would hand out a gift to one person at a time, starting with the youngest to the oldest. He explained to me that it was because it allowed everyone to appreciate what they got, and to show appreciation to the person who gave it to them.

I got several things that I really appreciated, it wasn't like the overtly grand and expensive items my parents would buy. They wouldn't put a lot of thought into such things, with Clemmy and Parker, I got things that they really put thought into. Things I actually needed, having moved into their home from my wealthy parents, without bringing many of my things.

Everyone seemed happy with the gifts and spent the day enjoying the small pleasures that came with having a happy family. Clemmy cheerily wore her new Tiffany jewelry while she made an extravagant dinner. Quail, Steak, Shrimp, and scallops with baked potatoes, asparagus, and corn on the cob. I'm told they changed up what they had for Christmas dinner every year, that sometimes it's like a thanksgiving dinner, with turkey and ham, and all the fixings. One year they had a taco dinner, where they had a huge taco selection, and everyone ate tacos.

I spent the day sitting with Zeb, enjoying the love and companionship he gave me. He was thoughtful, always noticing the little things about me, that I didn't even realize I was doing. I'd nibble at my long hair when I was nervous, and he would grab my hand and tell me it was okay. It was really nice, being noticed and adored the way he did me. Then, Emma brought out a board game, and I tried my hardest not to scowl. She would be a Debbie downer to my party plans with Zeb. Now he was going to go play board games with everyone, and I was going to be left all alone again. Ridiculous.

I stomped off to the room, noticed by everyone that I was having a small fit. No one commented and went about getting ready to play the new game that Des had gotten for Christmas. Everyone had gotten a different board game; this was to encourage the comradery between siblings.

Sitting in the room, I pulled out my phone and texted JP.

-Me: How was your Xmas?

-JP: Pretty good, parents spoiled me. They bought me a car. The perks of being an only child.

-Me: That sounds awesome. You want to know something?

-JP: Sure, what's up?

-Me: I think I still have a crush on you from all those years ago.

-JP: Really? I kind of feel the same way.

-Me: Really? I'm only with all these different guys to make you jealous.

-JP: It kind of worked.

-Me: I wish I could see you. I will find a way.

-JP: Not going to be possible, my parents got me on lock down.

-Me: Dang. Alright. Well, I got to go; I'll talk to you later.

-JP: Cya later.

-Me on Snap: Eli, what are you doing?

-Eli on Snap: Nothing.

-Me on Snap: I can't sneak out tonight, but Saturday is the new years party, and we are all going. Are you going to be there?

-Eli on Snap: If you're going, I'm not going. I don't want to see you after you left the things the way you did.

-Me on Snap: There were no things, Eli.

That night, lying next to Zeb, he fell asleep fairly fast. I lay there, wide awake. I decided I'd call and talk to one of the few girls that I knew. Zeb was asleep so I didn't have to worry about anything.

"Hey Trini, what are you doing?" I whispered.

"Hey Tanna, nothing at all. Just hanging out."

"Yeah? You still seeing that one girl? Felicity was her name, right?"

"Yes, that was her name and no, we broke up like a month ago."

"Dang what happened?"

"She said she was straight and wanted to see a man. I was just an experiment to her."

"That's freaking crazy!" I whisper-yelled.

"Yeah, her loss though, I'm the shit. What about you though, you still with Zeb?"

"Yeah, he just neglects me, maybe I should get me

189

a good girl to be with."

"Girl you are too damn straight for a girl."

"I am not straight; I am definitely gay. Plus, I'd rather be gay than deal with a boyfriend who is neglecting and ignoring me all the time."

Zeb rolled over in his sleep, not making a sound. I lowered my voice a little and Trini and I continued our conversation back and forth about me being straight for almost an hour. I noticed that Zeb was facing me, and I squinted a little and turned my phone to where the light could gently glance off his face. His eyes were open.

"I got to go." I quickly got off the phone.

"Hey babe, did I wake you? I'm sorry."

"I've been awake for an hour."

We didn't say another word to each other, until the next day. I slept fitfully, but I did sleep. When I got up in the morning, I felt down and sad. I knew I had been caught, and I wasn't sure how I was going to get out of it. Zeb was angry with me.

Zeb was up and off to work early the next day. He didn't kiss me bye or say anything to me. He just got dressed then left. I was concerned that my time as his girlfriend was coming to an end. I would have to try everything I could think of to fix this.

"Parker, I think Zeb is upset with me."

"Why? What happened?"

"Well, last night he was asleep, I was talking on the phone to one of my friends and I woke him up. He said, 'I've been awake for an hour.' Then didn't say anything else. Why didn't he just tell me he was awake and ask me to be quiet?" I tried to make it seem like it was all his fault.

190

Clemmy chimed in, "That's strange, I figured he would have asked you to be quiet."

Parker said, "Well wait a second, Zeb is super sweet, perhaps he was just hoping that you would realize he was trying to sleep and had to work in the morning, and just patiently waited for you to finish your phone call. Zeb is not a big fan of confrontation, but he will stand his own if need be."

Clemmy said, "That's true. I don't know, let's just ask him when he gets home, I have an idea, so Zeb's love language is acts of service, maybe if you showed him some acts of service, like cleaning his room that you helped destroy, he would respond well for you. Do you want to do that while he's at work? I bet it would really surprise him."

Emma said, "Yeah, you really should go clean that room, it's really bad."

I nodded, thinking that what they were saying was a good idea, I just wasn't going to be doing that. I don't clean rooms; I don't clean, period. I got up and wandered back to Zeb's room, making an appearance like I was going to go clean it.

When Zeb got home, he didn't say hi to me or anything, he just went straight to his room to decompress from his day at work. Parker got up and walked into his room. Five minutes later, Parker called me into the bedroom and sat me down on Zeb's bed.

"Okay here's the deal, Tanna you weren't being entirely honest with me earlier when you explained what happened between you and Zeb. First of all, he heard what you were saying about him to your friend. That isn't okay. Second of all, he heard you tell your friend that you were gay, and that you were being

191

neglected. These things just aren't true."

"I am bi-sexual!" I said, affronted.

"Tanna, Bisexual and being gay are not exactly the same thing. Can you not see how what you said could be hurtful to your boyfriend?"

"Yes, I do, I'm sorry Zeb. I never should have said anything about you to anyone. I messed up, I won't do it again. Please forgive me."

"Tanna, your friend Ruthelle was even overheard by Clemmy asking if Zeb was still neglecting you. Do you not see how this is not okay?"

"I didn't say that she said that on her own," I said, defensively.

"You allowed her to say that about your man. These are the kinds of things that you have to get under control, they aren't okay, and they are hurtful."

"I'm so sorry," I said, starting to cry.

"Zeb, do you love Tanna?"

"Yes dad, I really do."

"Tanna, do you love Zeb?"

"Of course, I do."

"You both love each other, awesome. Now I'm going to leave, you two fix your stuff. Tanna, apologize to him again, and Zeb, be open to forgiveness, if she's genuine, you can tell."

Parker left the room, and I apologized to Zeb again, more fervently and honestly. Zeb looked me in the eyes and said, "I love you. I forgave you immediately, it's okay. Don't worry about it."

"I love you too Zeb."

Chapter 25
The New Years Party

Almost every night that I had been living at the Fowlers residence I had done something for myself. Whether I was sneaking out to go be with Eli, or having phone sex with Lucky, sometimes I would just sit in the den and gorge myself on junk foods, I have gained almost twenty pounds since coming to live here. It has gotten harder to sneak about and do the things I wanted to do because I was now staying in the room with Zeb.

I never would have imagined that an eighteen year old boy would be so insistent that a beautiful seventeen year old girl wasn't lying in the bed with him all the time. I never imagined that that same boy wasn't going to be all over the opportunity of spending time with the girl he loved. I didn't understand love, I didn't understand that there are so many different kinds, I didn't even care about those other kinds. It was my kind that mattered.

Tonight was the same as the previous night, I had to lay there and toss and turn because my body was accustomed to being awake until the wee hours of the morning. Tonight, I lay here and listened to the slow rhythmic breathing of a sleeping Zeb, up on the bed.

I began to question my own thoughts; did I truly know how to get what I wanted? Hell, did I even know what I wanted? As I lay there, questioning the validity of my resolve, I felt my phone vibrate beneath me. Picking it up, I saw a message from Eli on Snapchat.

Eli on Snapchat: Hey, I'm thinking about you. This is usually the time I'm picking you up on the corner.

-Me on Snapchat: Yea it is. If I came outside, would you come get me?

-Eli on Snapchat: I'm already sitting here at the corner.

-Me on Snapchat: That's absurd.

-Eli on Snapchat: It's true. I was hoping you would be able to come out.

Just then I heard the soft shuffling and scuffle of footsteps from a heavy man walking down the hallway towards the kitchen. Parker must be up getting a snack or two for him and Clemmy. It occurs to me that the decompression time of adults with children is a far cry longer than one of a young adult who just has a job.

-Me on Snapchat: Not going to happen tonight. Parker is still up; Des is in the den and I'm laying in Zeb's room on the small bed.

-Eli on Snapchat: Well, I will wait, maybe they will go to sleep soon.

-Me on Snapchat: That's a good idea, you should wait there, if everyone falls asleep, maybe I will come out.

-Eli on Snapchat: Okay. Do you want a picture of me to keep you going while we wait?

-Eli on Snapchat: **Picture sent**

Eli had sent a picture of his junk. It was unkempt, untrimmed, and engorged. The picture was disgusting. I've seen so many other dick pics that this one wasn't impressive.

-Me on Snapchat: Thanks buddy. Just wait around for me, I'm going to check things out around the house.

I shut my phone off for the time being, fully intending on going to sleep. I was never going to go out and hang out with him, it just felt good to keep him hanging on.

I didn't have my phone off for more than a couple of minutes, before I powered it back on. I ignored the pop-up notifications from Snapchat and opened up my Tik Tok. I knew if I trolled through my messages long enough, I could get various dirty pictures sent to me from people all over the world. I got off on teasing these guys and knowing that they really wanted me.

After scrolling through dirty pictures of men, and sometimes women for hours, I fell asleep. I hadn't thought about Eli still sitting out there until the morning light came up, then I imagine he probably left after not getting a reply from me for over an hour. I didn't care either way.

The New Years party was coming up, Parker was very excited and so was Clemmy. It was a gathering of Parker's entire family, from his brothers and sisters to his mom and dad. Most of his nieces and nephews would be there as well. All the adults were going to be drinking and playing cards, until the new year rang in. The excitement was palpable.

I spent the day before the party just staying out of everyone's way. Zeb was playing on his computer with his friend Austin, while Emma and Payton played Spider-man on the TV in the living room. Des was outside goofing off with one of his neighborhood friends, playing with his new remote-control car he had gotten for Christmas.

I decided to hang out on Zeb's bed, thinking of a way I could get his attention. I could tell there was a distant barrier between the two of us now, probably because of the conversation I was having with Trini a few nights ago. I had an idea, which was messed up, almost as much as sleeping with his cousin. I was in a group text with Zeb, Eli, and Austin. They encouraged me to invite some of my friends there too, but I just didn't. If I invited other females, I would have to share the attention I got. It was possible that they would steal the eye from Zeb too. I wasn't about to risk all that.

I figured I would text Austin, privately. I knew that there was a chance I could have my cover blown, because Austin was the closest thing to a brother Zeb's own age, that Zeb had. Austin was his ride or die. I knew I would never meet Austin in person, unless I went to Omaha to visit Zeb's mom, when Zeb went. Still, it was always good to have doors open, plus, if I can pull Austin's attention away from Zeb, maybe Zeb will give me more of his attention. When Zeb hopped up and went to the bathroom, I realized this was a perfect time.

-Me: Hey Austin, what are you doing?

-Austin: Just playing a game with Zeb.

-Me: Cool. Hey, you saw those pictures of me, did you think I was pretty?

I cringed as I realized I sounded like a thirsty attention seeking tramp.

-Austin: Yes, I seen them, and sure, yeah, you're pretty.

-Me: Would you ever consider swapping pictures with me?

-Austin: What do you mean?

196

-Me: I mean, dirty pictures. I like to look at pictures of different people.

-Austin: Tanna, I'm going to say this one time, and one time only.

-Austin: Woman! If you do not halt thy attempts at undermining my best friend, by trying to seduce me, I will be letting him know immediately. I will laugh as thine memory is naught but ashes, spreading fitfully across the disgusting landscape you call your world. Even now, I may tell him your ways, as you are not fit for my brother, my best friend, Zeb!

-Me: I was just having a laugh, chill.

That night, I lay in my bed, unable to sleep again, thinking about what Austin had said to me. Can friendships be that strong? Surely if I was around him in person, I could have gotten him to crack his moral compass for me. It was probably just a distance thing. It definitely wasn't my fault.

The day of the New Years party was chaotic. With all the preparations from the day before being completed, it was about getting the things in the car and taken to Parker's little brother's house. The party was going to be held there.

When we got to Zeb's uncle's house, I noticed that they had a really nice house off in the woods, with a huge slightly sloping front yard. My eyes were immediately drawn to the three dogs that came loping out of the house when the front door was opened. A giant German Sheppard called Remington, a small weenie dog they called Stella, and a very small teacup chihuahua they called Peanut.

As I got closer to the covered porch, I noticed that the two smaller dogs were very old. The graying around their eyes and snout made this obvious. They still bounded and played like they were pups. I scratched them each behind their ears before heading towards the house.

Inside the house was a large family, full of smiling faces. As Parker and Clemmy made their rounds giving all of the various people hugs, and salutations. I was introduced one at a time to all the different family members.

Parker's dad stuck out to me; he was the oldest one there. His large body showed signs of the wear and tear that goes with being a life-long over the road truck driver. He had already had quite a bit of drink. It was clear he was feeling pretty good.

I sat down on the couch, while everyone else scattered into the various groups to hang out and be silly with. Parker and Zeb sat at the table and got dealt into the next hand of cards, Clemmy was hanging out with a couple of Zeb's aunts, Des went down the hallway, I assumed to play with the kids his age, and the Emma-Payton combo was goofing off with some of Emma's older cousins. Everyone had a place, except me.

I pulled out my phone and started texting JP.

-Me: Hey, what are you doing this new year's eve?

-JP: nothing, just playing games on my computer. You?

-Me: I'm at a party with Zeb's family. It's pretty cool, a lot of old people drinking and goofing off.

-JP: Sounds like fun.

-Me: Yeah. You don't have anyone to spend new year's with?

-JP: Nope, all alone here.

-Me: I'd come over if I could, but again, I'm stuck at the party.

-JP: It's all good, I would have had to sneak you in anyway.

-Me: Yeah, maybe another time.

After a few hours of everyone enjoying themselves, Zeb had come over and sat down with me for a little while and we hung out. All of Eli's siblings were there, but he didn't show up, just as he said. I decided I wanted to step outside and get a little of that cool fresh air, I was tired of being stuck inside.

When I walked outside, I saw Parker's dad, Allen. He was sitting on the front porch, smoking a cigarette and drinking a dark liquid out of a whiskey glass.

"Hey there little girl, what are you doing out here?"

"Hey there Mr. Fowler, I'm just getting some fresh air."

"Sho, you're…with my grandson, Zeb eh?"

I could tell he was on the verge of being too sloshed to be able to communicate, as his words were slurred, and drawn out.

"I am. I really love him."

"Good, Hesh a goodth kid."

"Yes, he is, it's cold out here, I'm going to go back inside."

I went back inside quickly, it didn't bother me that he was drunk, I just didn't want to have a conversation with him about Zeb. I had to figure out a way that I could leave here. Ideas were pouring through my head when I had one that I thought might work. I knew the kind of people Parker and Clemmy were, they were the kind to never victim blame, the kind that would remove one of their kids from a situation if there was any inclination that something toxic was happening.

"Clemmy, I don't feel comfortable. Mr. Fowler, Parker's dad, makes me feel really uncomfortable."

"What's the matter hon?"

I had pulled Clemmy aside, to where only she could hear me. I figured the easiest route for me to take was to make it appear that I was uncomfortable, and they would remove me from the situation.

"Well, he was making some really inappropriate statements when I was outside earlier, and now I don't feel comfortable."

I wanted to go see JP tonight, but step one would be to get everyone to leave the party before it was over. I would worry about step two when we got home. Hopefully, with Clemmy looking at me sadly, I could tell that she was trying to figure out what to do.

"I got an idea, you and I will go to the car and watch a movie, until Parker and Zeb are done here."

This idea wasn't going to work for me, so I said, "No that's okay, I'll just deal with it. I need to figure out how to handle these situations, or I'll run from everything in life. I don't want to be that way."

"If you're sure, I'll keep an eye out for you as well. Just stick near me then."

I was frustrated. The first attempt didn't work, I would have to take it a step further. I found a little bit of New Years confetti lying on the ground, took a quick look around and then licked it and stuck it to my cheek.

Step 1 is complete.

With the paper sprinkles sticking out obviously on my face, I walked towards the table. Clemmy had just gotten up and went to the bathroom, so I had a few moments to try. I went and stood next to old Mr. Fowler, where he was playing cards. Fortunately, Zeb was sitting to his right, the decorative trash was on my left cheek.

After a couple of moments, old Mr. Fowler looked up at me, because I made a particularly loud giggle when Zeb played his cards. There was no reason for the giggle, it was just for attention. Mr. Fowler saw the trash on my face, and without thinking, he reached up and brushed it off. I immediately backed away, as if horrified that he had tried to touch me. No one else seemed to notice.

I was fortunate that Clemmy was walking back down the hallway and witnessed the brush of the back of his hand against my cheek, and my visceral reaction. She immediately walked up to me, and grabbed my hand, pulling me out of the situation. After sitting there for a moment punching something on her phone, she looked at me and said, "Let's go sit in the car."

Cheering for joy inside, I nodded as if chastised and grabbed my shoes. Parker stood up, looked at Clemmy and said, "What's happening?"

"I'm surprised you didn't see it yourself babe."

"I didn't see anything."

"Check your phone, I explained what happened."

After looking at his phone, he looked at me, standing by the door. "Go outside Tanna, we will be there in a few minutes." He then looked around the room and made a blanket statement, "We are leaving. Zeb grab your stuff and go let your sister and little brother know."

Walking out the door, I had the biggest smile on my face. This was easier than I expected. I heard Parker talking to his brother as the door opened and Zeb came out to put his shoes on.

"Look, I don't want to leave either, but you know as well as I do that it's best for everyone if we just call it a night, and head home."

"You're probably right, but still, it bums me out because this was supposed to be a family event."

"I know, I'm sorry. I love you all!"

Parker climbed into the passenger seat of his car, and Clemmy pulled us out of the drive. He had been drinking a little bit, so he was not going to risk driving. I put on the waterworks and started forcing myself to hyperventilate. I had to pull out all the stops for this show to make it super convincing. I imagined that if a girl was touched inappropriately, she would be incredibly emotionally compromised.

"I feel so dirty," I wailed.

Parker said nothing, Zeb held my hand, and whispered, "It's going to be okay."

It was a little after 10:30 pm when we got home.

Chapter 26
A Sisters Fury

Me: It's almost the new year!

    -JP: I know! It's going to be a great year! This one wasn't great. Not the worst, but not great.

-Me: I'll text you after the ball drops.

It was 11:58 pm. I was laid up in bed with Zeb, we were both watching the ball count-down on his tv. I just knew he would be dedicating his attention to me, tonight. It was a new year, which was the way it was supposed to be.

10....

09....

08....

07....

06....

05....

04....

03....

02....

01....

"HAPPY NEW YEAR!" We both shouted together. We swept our faces towards each other, sharing in a deep new year's kiss. I loved this man. How could I not? After our kiss, he yawned really big.

"I'm sorry Tanna, I don't want to, but I have to go

to sleep. I have to work in five hours. If I had more seniority I could make the lowest man, do it, but since I'm the lowest man, it's not possible."

"It's okay Zeb, I totally understand."

I did understand, I just hated every single minute of it. Well, if he wasn't going to be giving me mine tonight, then I would get it from somewhere. I text JP.

-Me: Hey can I tell you a secret?

-JP: yea

-Me: I'm super horny right now.

-JP: Want to come over?

-Me: You said your parents wouldn't let you have anyone over.

-JP: They are all having a party, you could easily sneak in. You will just have to park on the road.

-Me: I'll see if I can.

I messaged Clemmy, making up a lie. She was going to be the one I had to convince to allow me to go. We still hadn't managed to get the guardianship paperwork taken care of, when we went to the notary, it was noticed that the dates on the paperwork were wrong, so we had to redo it all.

-Me: Clemmy, can I go to my friends' house? She lives about ten to fifteen minutes from here, she's having a really hard time dealing with the holidays.

-Clemmy: We don't feel comfortable with that, for several reasons. The first being that it's the most dangerous night of the year for drunk drivers. Another reason is that it's after midnight, and your curfew is 10 pm on the weekends. It's late, just give her a call or face time her then try to get some sleep.

-Me: Please Clemmy, I will be extra safe, and it's not very far from here. I promise, I won't be gone long.

-Clemmy: I'm sorry Tanna, It's just not safe.

I was furious. How could she lie in her warm bed and tell me that I can't go do something. She will be asleep in no time, then I'll leave anyway. Des is already asleep, Emma and Payton are in their room, and Zeb is also sleeping. It would be nothing for me to sneak out and go, then be back before anyone got up.

I got up about twenty minutes later, when I was sure no one else was going to be up and roaming through the house. I left very quietly through the garage door, not bothering with even checking that the camera was still turned. It had been turned on its side the last six times I had snuck out, and no one had bothered fixing it.

I got in my car and eased down the road, not revving up a lot, or causing any unnecessary noise. I was grateful I had a tiny car, that just didn't make a lot of noise. I messaged JP as I pulled out on the highway.

-Me: I'm on my way.

-JP: Good, text me when you get here, and I'll let you in the back door.

Fifteen minutes later, I pulled into a brand-new subdivision that was still being built. The house JP lived in was a huge house, similar to the size of the one my parents owned. There was a long driveway that curved a little. Everything was so new, there wasn't even grass on the sides of the road yet, it was just dirt and mud. I parked just out of view of JP's house, hopped out, locked my car, and then walked to JP's back door.

-Me: I'm here, I'm out back.

JP opened the back door, and we snuck up to his bedroom. I threw myself into his arms, right after he locked the bedroom door. I had been crushing on JP for almost three years now, and I was ready to get him on my list of trophies.

JP and I were lying together in his bed, naked. I was straddling him when suddenly his bedroom door erupted in a loud pounding noise. Someone was outside his door, trying to get in.

"JP! If you don't open this door this very second, I'm going to kick it in."

"JP, open the door."

It was JP's mom and dad outside the door. I quickly rolled off of him, grabbing my red skirt and throwing it on my body. I was searching around for my bra and shirt, when he looked at me with panicked eyes.

"Coming!" he said loudly to his parents. In a terrified whisper he said, "Hurry!" He got up, threw some shorts on, then walked to his bedroom door. I threw the shirt on without buckling my bra. The moment he unlocked the door, it flew open. There was a fuming man and a concerned woman standing in the doorway. They glared at me, and at their son.

"What the heck is this JP? Who is this?" JP's mom said, with a concerned voice and look.

"It doesn't matter, get dressed and get your shit girl, let's go."

Looking down, I realized my bra was hanging out of my shirt, unclasped and not looped through one arm. My panties were still hanging off of one leg, and my socks and shoes were nowhere to be seen. I was thoroughly embarrassed as JP's mom stood there watching over me as I put my clothes back on and walked out the bedroom door.

As Kevin, JP's dad, walked me out of the door, my

head hung even lower. There were the blue lights of a sheriff sitting down at the end of the driveway near where my car was, and several people standing around it. As we walked up to the scene, the sheriff was on the phone with someone, and I distinctly heard him say, "One moment ma'am."

Kevin said, "I found this unwanted guest in my home, I believe that it's her car."

"It is my car."

The sheriff spoke into the phone again, "Ma'am, there was a girl found, and she said it was her car, what do you want me to do with the car? Since it's registered to you as the owner, it's your call."

After the sheriff hung up the phone, he looked at Kevin and asked him a question, "You found her in your house? Did she damage anything?"

"No, she was upstairs dilly-dallying my son. We were alerted to her presence because they weren't exactly quiet with what they were doing."

"How old is your son sir?"

"He's fifteen. Barely."

"Do you want to press any charges on this girl for breaking and entering?"

"No, I don't think that's a good idea. Just take her home."

The sheriff turned to me, "What's your name young lady?"

"Tanna. I can just drive my car home."

"No, that's not going to happen, even if the neighborhood watch didn't let all the air out of your tires, I would be escorting you home, so I could talk to your guardian in person."

"Can I call her?"

"Of course, so that they are awake and can unlock the door."

After I climbed into the back of the police car, I pulled out my phone and called Clemmy. She answered after the third ring, "Hullo?"

"Clemmy, I'm being brought home by the police."

"What? Why? Are you okay?"

"Yes, I showed up to my friend's house and their parents were having a party, so there wasn't enough room in their driveway, so I parked in the dirt on the side. Then someone came along and popped all my tires."

"Okay. I'll see you soon."

I heard Parker in the background saying, "What's going on?" Then Clemmy hung up the phone.

The cop and I got to the house twenty minutes later, not saying a word to each other the entire trip. When we pulled into the driveway, I noticed Clemmy and Parker were standing out on the front porch, with their arms crossed. It was the exact picture I would think about, when a child got in trouble at school, and his parents just found out.

Walking up to the door Clemmy sternly said, "Go in the house Tanna."

I heard Parker saying something to the officer about coming inside where it was warm, then the three of them came into the house. Des was asleep in the Den, so I just went and sat on the couch. This wasn't going to be good, but I'll lie as much as I can to lessen the blow.

"What happened?"

The police officer told them exactly what happened, I found out that the meddling neighborhood watch

208

ruined everything for me.

"Well, it's New Years Eve, so most people were up enjoying themselves and having a party. Someone noticed the small dark colored car had pulled up by the driveway, shut off, then nothing. No one saw anyone get out, but they knew that car didn't belong in their neighborhood. They called everyone around the neighborhood, and no one said they knew anything about it, so they thought it was a burglar's getaway car. They then got the bright idea to let all the air out of the valve stems of each of the tires, which if you ask me, shows some situational genius. While that was going on, they called us at the sheriff's office and told us about it. It was then that the owner of the house she was parked near decided to search the inside of his home.

"When we got there, I called the owner of the car after running the plates. She said they owned a towing business and that her driver didn't live far from there. So, she sent a tow truck over to get the car. Around then, Kevin, the owner of the house where Tanna was, came up to me and told me they found an unwanted guest in their home in the bedroom of their fifteen-year-old male son. They did not want to press any charges for breaking and entering, so I just brought her home. I'm not going to make a report about this so that DHS doesn't have to get involved, but I wanted to let you guys know what was happening so that you can keep it inhouse."

"Thank you for bringing her home."

The sheriff turned and left, shutting the door behind him. The second it closed, Clemmy rounded on me. "You lied to me. You lied to all of us!"

I said, "I didn't mean to lie, if I would have told you I was going to a boy's house because he was being mistreated, but you would have told me no."

"We did tell you no. It was too late at night with the most drunk drivers on the road, all year. You disobeyed and went anyway. To top it all off, you betrayed Zeb, you went to see a boy. A fifteen-year-old boy! I don't want you dating my son anymore!"

"We didn't do anything; I just sat there and spoke with him about how he was feeling. Nothing more, and nothing less took place."

Parker spoke up for the first time, "You're lying. There's zero way you were just sitting in there doing nothing, in the middle of the night, with a boy."

I started crying, sniffling, and huffing loudly, "I can't believe you would accuse me of cheating on Zeb!"

"You did cheat on Zeb, Tanna." Parker glared at me. "You betrayed the sweetest, most dedicated man of my family."

"I would never cheat on Zeb, I love him. I wouldn't cheat on him at all!"

"Look Tanna, we aren't going to kick you out for this, don't worry about that. We told you we wouldn't, we meant that. You need to be prepared that in the morning, Zeb is not going to want to be in a relationship with you anymore. That's your new reality."

"Yeah, if he decides to forgive you, that's on him. I don't think he will."

"I'm going to encourage him that he shouldn't forgive you. You aren't a faithful trustworthy person, Tanna. I've known it for a long time."

I cried and nodded. Maybe this isn't going to be that bad. I lay back on the couch and kicked my feet up. Clemmy looked at me, shook her head sadly, then turned and went to her room. Parker looked at me in disgust then left the living room as well. As he passed by the room where the girls were supposed to be sleeping, he saw a couple of faces sticking out of the door. He whispered to them for a few seconds, then kept walking down the hallway. Emma's face narrowed at me, she squinted her eyes and I swear I could hear her growling. It would be an interesting day in the morning. I set my phone on the ground next to the couch, closed my eyes and easily drifted off to sleep.

Two hours later I was rudely woken up by Clemmy and Parker. I looked at Clemmy and she was holding my phone in her hand. If she had gone through my phone, that was it. I couldn't hide anything anymore.

"Your mom suggested I went through your phone, but I refused. I refused because I felt like I was violating your privacy, but I made a concession to her. I told her if you ended up doing something like breaking the law, then I would, and I would do whatever I could to get you back on track to being a positive contributing member of society."

Parker cut in, "Turns out, you have a thing for lying, and for sneaking around with all these different boys. You see Tanna, I have the same kind of phone that you do, whereas everyone else here other than Emma doesn't have that same kind, so they don't know how to use it the way you and I do. Unfortunately for you, I knew just where to go and what to do to find your deleted messages. You have no less than four boyfriends, or boys that you're fooling around with. You have full on picture exchanges with grown men, 47-year-old men. In fact, I'm getting Zeb up right now, and we are going to have all of this out in the open at this very moment."

He walked towards the hallway and opened Zeb's bedroom door. I didn't hear what he said to Zeb, but the tone of it was very caring and loving.

Zeb came into the living room and sat down, away from me, in between Parker and Clemmy.

"Zeb, we have some bad things to tell you, it's going to be very hard to hear, and I'm sorry for having to do it this way. Tanna has been sleeping with several different boys, tonight she was brought home from a boy named JP's house, by the police. Lucky has been her boyfriend this entire time, and they were always more than just support group members."

Zeb was physically shaking, his entire body shuddering and thick tears built under his eyes, before breaking and streaming quickly down each of his cheeks. I just stared at Zeb, and knowing there was no way to save the position I was in, I just smirked. I reveled in the feelings he was putting on display, the perfect man, the perfect boyfriend, gentle and easy to love, broken. My handiwork always brought a smile to my face, and right now the smile on my face was enough to put Clemmy over the top.

"You thought you could come in here and hurt MY SON!? YOU THOUGHT YOU COULD COME IN HERE AND DESTROY MY FAMILY!?"

"Yes, that's exactly what I thought," I said, with a small laugh.

"GIRL! I WAS RAISED IN THE GHETTO, MY

BLOOD IS GHETTO. I WILL BE DAMNED IF I LET SOME IMPOTENT CHILD COME IN HERE AND TEAR DOWN THE WALLS I HAVE BUILT WITH MY HUSBAND! YOU USED AND CHEATED ON MY SON!? HOW DARE YOU!?"

It was at this moment the first door in the hallway exploded open, the savage scream of a raging animal erupted with the slam and pound of the door against the wall. Emma came flying out of the room in a terrifying blur. I knew that I was about to pay physically for some of the things I had done.

Emma came running up to me, grabbed me by my hair and threw me to the ground. She immediately jumped onto my chest, knocking the air out of me. Straddling me, she began to unleash a hail of punches. They varied from hammer punches to hooks. She jumped up, turned to Payton, a savage grin on her face, almost beckoning Payton to join in on the carnage. Clemmy grabbed Payton in a rush of speed, telling her that she could not help Emma. She could not do anything, because Payton was over the age of eighteen, and the two fighting girls were both minors.

Emma stood there, allowing me to have a chance to stand up. I looked around, tears streaming down my face. I was alone in this world, no one was going to be here to save me. I would have to fight this fight as if I would never be saved by anyone, ever again.

I balled my fists up and glared at Emma. I taunted her, "I'll ruin his perfect little life, and there's nothing you can do about it."

Emma squared her stance and raised her fists the way her father taught her. She was going to make this girl suffer. With a quick step forward, Emma made a quick jab followed by a straight punch with her right hand. They both landed, snapping my head back. I felt the blood rolling out of my nose, my already too big for my face nose was now broken, flattened against my skin. I fell then, to my knees, utterly defeated.

Emma was about to come in for a finishing blow, when her dad grabbed her around her shoulders. "No sweetheart enough is enough. Give us the room please."

She looked at me and said, "You don't deserve someone like my brother. You deserve far worse." She turned on her heel and stormed back into the bedroom, Payton right behind her with a grin on her face. Zeb had gotten up and went to his room right after the fight had started, he didn't want to see any of this.

Chapter 27
Aftermath

Parker helped me to my feet and handed me a cold rag wrapped around ice for my face. "Here, this will help the swelling. I do have a question for you Tanna, something that I have been curious about."

"What?" I said, with a furious glare.

He looked at me coldly, with no emotion on his face. "I still don't know where you went, on the day you disappeared with Clemmy's car. Since everything is out in the open now, feel free to tell me."

I smiled at him, showing my bloody teeth. "Wouldn't you like to know."

"Yes, I would. That's why I asked."

I thought about it for a moment, and realized I could get one more quick stab into Zeb's heart. I would take his cousin and best friend away from him. I would break him completely, and he would never recover. Smiling, I said, "I was with Eli."

"Eli? As in my nephew Elisha?"

I nodded, grinning even bigger.

"I don't believe you. You have proven yourself a liar. Prove it to me."

"Look at my Snapchat. All his messages are deleted."

Sighing, he said, "That doesn't prove anything Tanna."

"Call him then."

"Alright, I will."

He called Eli from his phone, and asked him point blank, "Did you have sex with Tanna?"

"What?" he said groggily.

"She said you and her were having a fling, is this true?"

"What Uncle Parker? NO that's not true, I don't know what she's talking about."

"That's all I needed to know, thank you Eli. Here, talk to Zeb, he's going through it right now, and he needs a friend."

I listened and thought that Eli was a worthless scumbag. Of course, he would deny everything. I said, "I am not lying, we really did. In fact, almost every single night since I met him, I've been sneaking out of the house through the side door, he's been picking me up on the corner over there, and he's taken me to the library, and fucked me."

Parker stared at me, trying to decipher if I was lying or telling the truth. After a few minutes, he stood up, walked into Zeb's room, grabbed the phone back from Zeb and walked into his own room. I didn't hear what happened, but when Parker came back to the living room, he looked at Clemmy and said, "She's telling the truth about that, Eli just confirmed it. He's going to tell Zeb."

Parker was vividly fuming, he was shaking so hard, he couldn't hold his cup of tea.

"Zeb is the best of the men in my family. He's the kindest, and most gentle. He didn't deserve what you did to him. You disgust me, Tanna. I'm going to call your parents and tell them to come get you. You're not welcome here anymore."

Parker grabbed his phone and called my mom, when he got no answer, he gave my dad a call. My dad answered the phone, and I could hear Parker's side of the line. "Hello sir, I wanted to give you an update as to what happened last night, and where we are at with things...."

Parker had walked out of the living room towards his bedroom, and I lost track of what he had said after that. When he returned, he looked at Clemmy and said, "Her parents don't want her to move back in with them. They said we should refer her to DHS."

"Okay, I'll make some calls."

I didn't know what to think about that, my mom and dad said they didn't want me back. I stood up, and shouted, "I will not get in any car with a damn Fed!"

"Tanna, we have finished our discussion with you, you may sit there and be silent until someone comes to get you. Zeb will get your things packed up."

"I want to talk to my dad! Let me call my dad right now!"

"I will text your dad for you and see if he wants to speak with you. You are not getting any of these phones right now, I will return the phone your parents are paying for, to them."

Parker texted my dad, a few moments later he said, "Your dad doesn't want to talk to you Tanna. He said that because of his love for you, he will be manipulated by you into giving you everything you want. He doesn't think it's a good idea until you get some help."

"I don't believe you! LET ME TALK TO MY DAD! LET ME CALL MY DAD!"

Parker showed me the text message, and it instantly

cut my screams off. My dad didn't want to talk to me because of my mom. She was the real alpha in my home. I didn't know what to do, so I stood there, heaving.

Glaring at Clemmy, who was standing in the living room, I yelled, "I'm going to kill all of you." I rushed forward into the kitchen and tried to grab the big butcher's knife that Parker used to chop up sausages. Before I could get my short chubby fingers around it, Clemmy gave me a little boop with her hip, bumping me slightly off course. She knocked the big knife off the counter and into the sink, then turned and placed herself between the kitchen utensils and me.

"Get out of my way."

"Girl, that's exactly what I needed to hear you say. I'm calling the police."

Clemmy called the police, swapping places with Parker. I hobbled back into the Den and flopped down heavily on the bed. I didn't want to leave. I didn't want to give up my freedom. I didn't want to go back into the system.

I started crying, "Everyone always leaves me, I'm always alone. You guys are just like everyone else."

Within a minute of calling the police, they walked through the front door. It was a tall fit policewoman, her hair in a tight ponytail. She walked straight up to me and crouched down.

"Hey there, it's Tanna right? Are you okay?"

"Yes."

"I'm Officer Lane, I'm here to help you figure things out, okay?"

"Yes ma'am."

"Can you tell me what's going on?"

I told her the truth, I told her how I didn't want to go back into a group home, and that I didn't want to leave this place. I liked it here; they were nice and I loved them. I told her that I couldn't help myself.

"Who hit you? I see you have bruises on your face."

"I got in a fight with his daughter. She's the same age as me. It was my fault, I started it."

"Okay, no worries, no one is going to get in trouble for it."

Around this time, a slew of other police officers, EMT, and firemen came into the home. Parker and Clemmy sat on the couch, welcoming them all graciously. They asked them an assortment of questions, and then a male officer came and approached Officer Lane.

"I got the number to her adopted father, the one who has guardianship over her. Do you want to call or me?"

"I will. Tanna, I'm going to step outside and call your dad, okay?"

"Okay, can you get my phone from Parker? He won't give it back to me."

Parker stepped up, produced the phone from his pocket, and handed it to the police officer. "I told her I would give it to her parents, and they could decide when she got it back."

"No problem, we will make sure they get it."

A short while later, Officer Lane came back in and got down low again. "Here's the deal Tanna, I spoke with your dad and mom, they want to have you sent to Conway Regional to have you given a mental health evaluation. Afterwards, they will meet us at the hospital, and we will go from there, okay?"

"Okay."

"Do you want to ride with me? Or in an ambulance?"

"I'll ride with you; can we ride in the back of an ambulance please? I'm scared of police cars."

"Of course."

Without looking back at the family that had housed me, and cared for me for the last two months, I left the house, climbed into the back of the ambulance, escorted by Officer Lane. With a sudden finality, the ambulance doors slammed shut, putting an end to this chapter of my life.

Epilogue

The handsome nurse with the gray eyes came into my room again, checking my vitals and making sure I received my medication. I looked at him, wondering how old he was, and if he liked them younger. I bet I could seduce him, if I really tried. I shouldn't though, because if I did that, they would never release me from here if I got caught, or he turned me down.

It had been a week since I was put into the mental wing at the hospital. I have been taking my medicine and going to all of my therapy sessions and group counseling meetings. I think I could be released by next Monday if I maintain the good behavior. That's what I had to do, in order to convince my mother that I had made strides for the better.

Every day I sat around, or lay down, or stood there, leaning against a wall. Every single day, I would think about just how I was going to be able to get back at the Fowlers for taking away the most important thing in the world to me. My own freedom. I knew how to get into their home, I knew the days that no one was around at the house. I knew everything I needed to know to create a world of hurt for that family. Zeb was probably so broken, he couldn't function. I imagine he was sitting around the house, crying and weeping. The thought of him being miserable and broken kept me going while I worked with the hospital mental health staff. I would find out more when they released me.

I got released on a Monday, which meant I would be going to school on a Tuesday. My mom was still adamant that I be controlled completely. She kept insisting that I was going to be put in a residential inpatient care facility, but who knows.

Before school on Tuesday, my mom pulled me aside and told me that, "Zeb put your backpack in the office. It'll be at the school when you get there."

When I got to school, I waited until after first period, because I knew Zeb showed up late to school because of his class schedule. I then went to the office and requested to speak to the principal. I saw my backpack sitting in the corner by the front desk but ignored it.

"Zeb Fowler stole my backpack and won't give it back."

"We will page him."

Within five minutes, Zeb walked through the door of the front office, and without looking at me spoke firmly, but in complete control, "The backpack is right there." He pointed right at my backpack, not even acknowledging my presence. I could hear the anger and resolution in his voice. He had nothing for me, and I had no way of ever changing that. Zeb was done with me, I lost.

Three weeks later, my mom put me in a residential for mental health. I was to remain here until I turned eighteen, then I would be re-evaluated, and they would determine if I was a danger to myself or others. I would bide my time, I knew exactly what I wanted, and I knew how to get it.

*** The day Tanna left***

Zeb sat in his room, on the edge of the small twin bed that used to be Tanna's, throwing trash and clothes alike into a big black trash bag. Parker came into the room to check on his son. "Hey son, are you okay?"

"Yeah dad, I'm going to be okay. I'm just going to get all of her stuff put in these bags, and then set on the porch."

"I'll go grab some of the big boxes outside, we can use those too."

Together, Zeb and Parker went outside and grabbed some of the large amazon boxes that were set out for recycling and brought them inside. They would place all of Tanna's things in them, tape them up, and set them on the porch, so that they can be delivered to Tanna's parents' house.

During the excavation of Tanna's items, they found disgusting bloody underwear, mixed in with hundreds of little wrappers and trash from a dozen different types of cakes and candies. Zeb threw everything into the box, everything except for a small blanket, that said, 'Tanna Loves Zeb.'

"What are you saving that for?"

"Because she doesn't get to have this dad, she doesn't get to have anything that has my name on it. I'm going to burn it."

Nodding, Parker said, "I'm so sorry you had to go through this son, let's make sure we put everything that belongs to her in these boxes, I don't want anyone trying to say we are thieves."

An hour later, Parker stepped into Zeb's room. "Hey, I'm going to take all these boxes and stuff up to

Tanna's parents' house and drop them off in their garage. That's where they told me to put them. I know it's tough, but could you help me?"

"Yeah dad, of course I'll help you."

Parker noticed that Zeb didn't look too down, he didn't look too miserable and out of it. "You good boy?"

"Yeah dad, I think I'm going to be okay. I think… I think that I would have been hurting more, if I was more ready for a relationship. I don't think I was ready. I had been on the fence about her for a little while anyway, for the last week I had woken up and seen her looking at dick-pics, but I convinced myself I was just having a bad dream, so I rolled over and went back to sleep. What hurt me the most was Eli's betrayal. I think I will forgive him someday, but it's going to be a while. He seemed genuinely upset and down on himself because of what he was doing."

"I think he's upset because he got caught son, not because he did it."

"Still, it won't do me any good by harboring hate towards him. I just will go a while without talking to him, or spending time with him. Maybe he will mature and learn the value of family and friendship in that time. I love you dad, I'm really grateful that you're here with me. I think I'm good, after we get back from dropping all of this stuff off, I'm going to go bowling."

The End.

Acknowledgements

First and foremost, I want to thank my wife, Naomi. She put up with my crabbiness and sometimes belligerent acceptance of criticism while I wrote. She offered up some of the best advice a man could ask for, thank you for being my sounding board. I love you.

Secondly, I want to thank my daughter, she's inspired me through all of this, reading every word and encouraging me the whole time. You're one of my best friends. I love you, Emma.

Thirdly, I am thankful to my boys, Zeke, Desmond, and Ronan. You three are the foundation of love that exists within me. I couldn't do anything that I do without the beautiful family that I have. You're amazing. I love you boys.

Lastly, my dear readers. Your engagement through Patreon has really encouraged me to keep writing, watching the views tick up, more and more every day was both exiting, and scary. I am not the best writer, but I definitely enjoy it. Thank you.

About the Author

S am Toller is 37 years old; he works full time as a maintenance man for one of the local industrial plants, attends school full time for business, and is a loving husband and father. Sam began his young life as a member of a large family, with more than seven kids in the house at any given time. The struggles of being the middle child of such a large group of children were not zero, but the unity the family had developed has persevered through their entire lives. Sam is a family man, through and through.

www.ingramcontent.com/pod-product-compliance
Lightning Source LLC
Chambersburg PA
CBHW020446130626
46549CB00001B/319